Put the
Blame on
EVE

Put the Blame on Eve

What Women Must Overcome to Feel Worthy

Melinda J. Rising, Ph.D.

Larson Publications
Burdett, New York

ISBN-10: 1-936012-47-2
ISBN-13: 978-1-936012-47-3
Library of Congress Control Number: 2010933249

Publisher's Cataloging-In-Publication Data
(Prepared by The Donohue Group, Inc.)

Rising, Melinda J.
   Put the blame on Eve : what women must overcome to feel worthy /
Melinda J. Rising.

   p. ; cm.

   Includes bibliographical references and index.
   ISBN-13: 978-1-936012-47-3
   ISBN-10: 1-936012-47-2

   1. Misogyny--Religious aspects--Christianity. 2. Women in Christianity--
History. 3. Sex discrimination against women--Religious aspects--Christianity.
4. Women in popular culture--United States. 5. Equality--Religious aspects--
Christianity. 6. Eve (Biblical figure) I. Title.

BV639.W7 R57 2010
270.082   2010933249

Published by Larson Publications
4936 NYS Route 414
Burdett, New York 14818 USA

larsonpublications.com

19 8 17 16 15 14 13 12 11 10

10 9 8 7 6 5 4 3 2 1

Mixed Sources
Product group from well-managed forests and other controlled sources
www.fsc.org Cert no. SW-COC-002283
© 1996 Forest Stewardship Council

To Roland and Norma Werther,

loving parents who taught me the value of equality, truth, and dignity, and all

the strong women who have inspired me.

Contents

Acknowledgments

When a person embarks on a quest for answers that results in a nonfiction book, there are many champions on the journey who help inspire and shape the outcome. *Put the Blame on Eve* truly took a community to complete: many categories of people to whom I owe a debt of gratitude.

Longtime friend and mentor Dr. Kathleen Mc Grory has kept me in touch with the evolving status of women. A medieval scholar and researcher, her perspective has enlightened me and offered so much inspiration throughout the process. The works and friendships of Margaret Starbird, Dr. Karen Ralls, and Ani Williams also played integral roles in the outcome. Mary Magdalene, early Christian leader and activist, provided the connectivity among that illustrious group.

My acknowledgments should also include three authors from whom I drew heavily. Although I never knew the great mythologist Joseph Campbell, his knowledge and perspective on Eve gave me insights I hadn't thought of. I hope one day to meet Elaine Pagels, a brilliant biblical scholar whose books *Adam, Eve, and the Serpent*, *The Gnostic Gospels*, and *Beyond Belief* clarified my thoughts and filled in some blanks. And finally, I drew many details about Christianity and its evolution from *A History of Christianity* by Paul Johnson.

Discovering Matilda Joslyn Gage during my research was a stroke of good luck. This remarkable nineteenth-century suffragist surely played a role as "Muse" from the great beyond. Her book, *Woman, Church and State*, was so far ahead of its time!

Reference librarians have also helped elicit some difficult pieces of information. My colleagues at Three Rivers CC and Northwestern Connecticut CC along with those from the University of Connecticut Regional Campuses at Greater Hartford, Waterbury, and Torrington willingly provided me with needed obscure details when I was tearing my hair out.

During the process of conducting focus groups, I needed participants, venue hosts, and facilitators in locations far from my home. I'd like to extend special thanks to UCONN/Greater Hartford and UCONN/Stamford for providing space and enthusiasm for the project. Dear friends who played leadership roles in focus groups included Bonnie Rogers, who organized and arranged for the Mystic, Connecticut, group; Muriel Dickinson who organized and hosted the Narragansett, Rhode Island, group; Attorney Debra Smith Arthur who organized, hosted, and facilitated the Portland, Oregon, group; and Kaye Delano who organized, hosted, and facilitated the group at Amelia Island, Florida. Focus groups would not have been possible without them and their commitment to investigating the status of women.

Carol Virostek, past president of AAUW Connecticut, provided me with some wonderful background information and introduced me to two teenage women who had some definite opinions about women's history and the lack of information regarding inclusion of women's historical contributions in school curricula. Interviewing them added to my perspective. The AAUW (American Association of University Women) mission is advocacy for women and girls. I can embrace that mission!

I would be remiss not to mention the many contributions of time and energy of my agent and friend, Paul Cash, who bought into my message of balance and gender equality at that author/agent introductory session in New York City nearly a decade ago.

Finally, I am humbled by the many cheerleaders who have supported me along the way:

My family, especially my daughters Donalee and Shannon;

Commission friends, Margaret, Carole L., Roberta, Sister Joanne, Sheila, and Joy;

Deans Council Colleagues;

Magdalene Circles and fellow pilgrims to France, England, and Scotland;

Seeker Sisters;

Colleagues/friends REB, Gwendolyn, Pattie O., Margot, Gloria S., Edna, Phyllis, Diane;

UCONN PhD pals, Dr. Karen and Dr. Ruth;

And a few very special men.

And so we have it. With the help and support of all those named and some I may have inadvertently omitted, *Eve* has come to fruition. It was my job to investigate, inform, and raise awareness about where women stand in the scheme of things in our country. Readers will no doubt discern what is significant for them.

Prologue: The Scapegoat

Scapegoat. A powerful word.

It evokes an emotional, even visceral reaction from anyone who has been victimized as one.

Derived from a tale in the Hebrew Bible, scapegoating has come to mean irrationally blaming an individual or group for an act or disaster. It implies manipulating information to discredit a person or group. Blaming a minority group for the demographic or economic woes of a larger one is a far too common example. How easy, how convenient, to point the finger at others to avoid accountability for one's own actions!

The Old Testament story is of two male goats and a bull being offered as sacrifice in the temple in Jerusalem (Leviticus 16:3–28). Lots were cast to determine which goat would be a burnt offering along with the bull. The remaining goat would be the "scapegoat" to be banished to the wilderness, bearing the burden of guilt for mankind. New Testament theology has its own deeply poignant version of scapegoat in the form of Jesus who, having been driven into the wilderness by the high priests, took on the guilt of mankind.

The Scapegoat Society, formed in England in 1997 to study "scapegoating" and its effects on those implicated, defines the practice in this way:

> Scapegoating is a hostile social-psychological discrediting routine by which people move blame and responsibility away from themselves and towards a target person or group. It is also a practice by which angry feelings and feelings of hostility may be projected, via inappropriate accusation, towards

others. The target feels wrongly persecuted and receives misplaced vilification, blame and criticism; he is likely to suffer rejection from those whom the perpetrator seeks to influence. Scapegoating has a wide range of focus: from "approved" enemies of very large groups down to the scapegoating of individuals by other individuals. Distortion is always a feature.

Put the Blame on Eve looks deeply into Eve's perceived culpability for the Fall of Man, her resulting role as scapegoat, and how this conviction has determined the status of women for millennia. How did the conviction arise in the first place? Why has it prevailed? What role has "spin" played through the centuries, as different groups twisted the same information to elicit very different responses, depending upon their agenda?

My own "agenda" is not to elevate one gender over another. It is to equalize the roles gender plays, with an eye toward finding an optimal balance between them on this dynamic, volatile, and rapidly changing globe we share.

Toward this end, it is important to see how Eve and, by extension, women have been used as a scapegoat for millennia. It is important to see *exactly* how the established interpretation of the Garden of Eden account elevates men and subjugates women. It is important to see the extent to which such beliefs are responsible for the sexism and intolerance that persist today.

Fact, Faith, and Discernment

Finding truth about these things is not easy. While historical information is usually viewed as factual and truthful, we should not confuse history with fact. History is presented as truth, but clearly is a story told with the bias of a winner running all through it—informed and framed by the culture of the era. Rarely do we hear the perspective of the losers or the oppressed. Legends accepted as factual often possess only an element of truth, which has been exaggerated and embellished over time.

Doctrines taken on faith do not require proof or explanation to "believers," and often cannot be explained with logic or fact. In organized religion, dogma often must be believed without proof—the Church has declared it true and demands "faith" in its teachings. Submitting to such a demand can be very comforting to people who are searching for the Promised Land and feel that they can't possibly find their way without direction from organized religion. It may even bring or accompany an experience of something spiritual or mystical. But all too often it also requires forfeiting our prerogative of discernment, as the very effort to exercise it may be perceived as heretical.

In contrast, information meant to be taken as factual should be documented by verifiable date, artifact, and unbiased witnesses whenever possible. Anyone who has witnessed an accident knows, for example, that five separate observers will provide differing and sometimes conflicting accounts. Police look for the pieces of information that are most consistent. Without the benefit of actual documentation, circumstantial evidence concerning historical "fact" provides only *clues*. These clues help us determine possible truth, but our deductions are not necessarily conclusive. Careful discernment is needed.

People who employ discernment use their personal values and biases as parameters, determining which information to believe and retain and which information to discard. The process and parameters can vary dramatically from person to person, as "truth" determined by discernment does not derive its meaningfulness from external authority.

In my own case, I essentially believed for many years what I was told about historical facts and religious truth, doctor's diagnoses, legal advice, car sales information, and so on. I preferred to believe in the best in people, trusting that most are sincere. I tended to overrule a persistent subconscious acknowledgement that people often do have agendas and promote them passionately.

During the early 1960s, my college experience drew me into the civil rights movement for women and minorities; but activism soon was put on hold as a teaching position, marriage, and motherhood consumed my time, thoughts, and perspective. With the onset of middle age I endured a series of psychological and physical "crises." In the course of two years, I experienced major surgery, a divorce, a dissertation defense, selling my home, starting a new job, and having an empty nest with both my daughters away at college. Those events prompted some serious soul-searching for me as I attempted to determine my true identity, my life's purpose, and the means to accomplish it.

Questions long buried in the recesses of my brain began to surface. I wondered about the inequities in society, its prejudice and bigotry. Why are sexism and racism tolerated in a free country? Why does religious intolerance still prevail? Through much research I discovered many answers and far more questions. What I've learned so far has been both enlightening and disturbing, sparking my own personal flame of passion.

As my questioning and discernment transformed into a genuine Grail Quest, I began to focus on the role of women in early Christianity—perhaps as the result of my status as matriarch in a family of all females. That may also account for why Mary Magdalene became my passion. I was fascinated by the possibility of her significant leadership role as Apostle to the Apostles.

Although I am not a biblical scholar, I read volumes of information written by people who have dedicated their lives to such study. I was struck early on by works of feminist biblical scholars that present intriguing non-establishment interpretations, illuminated by the Gnostic gospels and other documents discovered in the twentieth century. In addition, I was blown away by stumbling upon the work of nineteenth-century suffragist Matilda Jocelyn Gage whose book, *Woman, Church and State,* was a hundred years ahead of its time. I also was struck by the work and courage of Margaret Starbird, as well as the research and insights found in Dan Brown's blockbuster *The DaVinci Code.*

Few people are aware, for example, that Mary Magdalene was exonerated by the Roman Catholic Church in 1969 from her erroneous title of penitent whore. My unofficial, informal poll of people I meet reveals that most Catholics have no idea that Magdalene had been wrongly labeled. Then again, newspapers rarely put retractions on the front-page either.

Why was the credibility of Mary Magdalene and other females dismissed? Why were misogynists allowed to influence so strongly the developing doctrine in organized religions and cultures?

All roads in my research led to the Garden of Eden and the reputed "Fall of Man" —in which Eve succumbed to the wiles of the serpent, dragging Adam screaming and hollering to bite into the fruit of the tree of knowledge. Ah, that must be it! All women are guilty because of an action of *one* woman, albeit the first woman, in a myth, a metaphor.

• • •

More and more modern writers speak of history as "his story"—a story that has discounted females, the feminine perspective, and the roles women have played through time. An objective researcher simply has to wonder how "history" might be portrayed differently if the feminine role and perspective were included. How might the role of contemporary woman look today if "history" had gotten it right? We will do some of that wondering here.

MJR

September 2010

1

Out of the Garden: Seduction, Sex, Sexism, and Original Sin

It is understandable that ancient cultures pondered their origins and created explanations for them. Scholars indicate that many of the earliest beliefs embraced the Mother Goddess concept, an obvious deduction since women gave birth to new life. Subsequent explanations, however, replaced the Mother Goddess with an all-powerful God and a patriarchal perspective. Creation stories were colorful and at times contradictory, but stories explaining the woes of humankind and death provided the basis for the negative status of women and spins that persisted for millennia.

Enter Eve . . .

Millions of people believe that mankind's "Fall from Grace" was the direct result of seduction and disobedience of the first man and woman. The serpent, long associated with the sacred feminine and symbolic of change and rebirth, initiated the seduction—which, as the story goes, was carried out by Eve. Conscious and subconscious internalization of this tale for centuries has condemned both serpent and woman in the dominant Western psyche, continuing through the modern era.

Sin was born. Was it the sin of disobedience . . . or of sex?

It began in the Garden, according to many ancient cultures struggling to explain the origins of life and the phenomena of nature and its challenges. Judeo-Christian tradition calls it "the Garden of Eden," a perfect place of beauty, peace, and harmony without contrast or negatives, void of hunger, stress, pain, anguish, and death. Time did not exist.

The Seduction

A friend with whom I discussed the premise of this book mused at the Garden of Eden scenario as it might have unfolded in a reality show:

> *"Adam, honey, I'm tired of watching the grass grow. Let's check out the fruit the Serpent showed us on the Tree of Knowledge."*
>
> *"I don't know, Eve, God warned us about that tree."*
>
> *"Aren't you curious, Adam? We need a little adventure!"*
>
> *"Ho, hum, Eve. I am a little bored, no offense."*
>
> *"There it is. It looks so sweet and juicy. Just one little tug . . . Come on, Adam, take a bite."*
>
> *"After you, Eve. Wow, this is great!"*
>
> *"Oh my gosh, Adam. Now I know what THAT's for!"*
>
> *Adam and Eve, knowing at that moment that they were indeed different from one another, sought fig leaves to cover their private parts—which was a dead give-away to God. They were thus banished from the Garden of Eden to live in a land of opposites.*

So much for the musing. What does it mean?

How should we interpret the Garden of Eden story? Myth? Legend? A metaphor or allegory? Historical fact? These questions have long been discussed and debated by scholars and theologians. Fervent believers even in twenty-first-century Judeo-Christian tradition might feel that a scene similar to the "reenactment" above actually happened and would attribute the miseries of humanity to the weaknesses and seduction of the first man and woman.

But how was it that Eve alone became ultimately accountable? How would that belief shape future attitudes against women? How would it influence our feeling of revulsion toward our bodies? What was the sin committed here?

The Hebrews originally considered the sin to be one of disobedience. How and when did the nature of that sin change in people's minds to sex? Let's explore how and when that transition took place and how it impacted the evolving Church.

Many experts have taken up the issue of how cultures, in particular the Hebrews, came to their conclusions about the so-called Fall and its consequences. Joseph Campbell, highly respected mythologist and professor at Sarah Lawrence College, discussed various aspects of the "Fall of Man" in a series of interviews with Bill Moyers featured on PBS. According to Campbell, nearly all early cultures have origin-of-life creation stories, and most also have included the "Fall of Man" component. The Judeo-Christian tradition, however, is to his knowledge the only culture to view the serpent as evil and to hold Eve responsible for the Fall. Campbell claims that other cultures view the serpent in a positive fashion, symbolizing throwing off the past and continuing to live.

During the interview, Moyers inquires why Eve is blamed for the Fall and why subsequent generations of women have been held accountable for her action. The explanation, according to Campbell, is that women are responsible for life: "They [women] represent life. Man doesn't enter life except by woman, who brings us into a world of pairs of opposites and suffering."

Campbell cited a possible historical explanation for that negative interpretation—the Hebrew subjugation of the Canaanites who worshipped the goddess. Their goddess was closely associated with the serpent which represented the mystery of life. Campbell felt there was an "historical rejection of the Mother Goddess implied in the Garden of Eden."

When the Hebrews plundered the Canaanites, they also crushed the worship of their goddess. The symbolism of suppressing the goddess would establish the supremacy of the Hebrew male deity while elevating the male status and supporting the rationale for masculine domination and patriarchy. The Hebrew interpretation of the creation story held Eve responsible for the Fall and further justified their assumption of male superiority. Extending the guilt to all women ensured continued subjugation of women through times to come. Eve became a convenient scapegoat and, as in any good curse, all her sisters would suffer along with her.

Some writers feel that the story of the Fall was not just *interpreted* to empower the male but was *deliberately devised* to undermine the power of the goddess and Earth Mother in order to elevate the patriarchal agenda. In *When God Was a Woman*, for example, Merlin Stone delineates a scholarly and revealing account of the decline of the goddess and the matrilineal society. She demonstrates through historical and archaeological sources how the Israelites—through their male god Yaweh (Jehovah)—intentionally trampled and undermined worship and reverence of the goddess for reasons other than monotheism, the reason usually cited for their actions. Like Campbell, she also discusses in some detail the Fall of Man(kind) as represented in many cultures, most of which apply different spins to the same basic theme. According to Stone, it is only the Judeo-Christian tradition which succeeds in the degradation of Eve and, by association, all women. In her book *At the Root of This Longing*, Carol Lee Flinders adds that as a result of demonstrating women's vulnerability and perceived weakness, Hebrew as well as Greek views would justify women's exclusion from all institutions (Flinders, p. 117).

The Punishment

To the woman [God] said, "I will greatly multiply your pains in childbirth, In pain you will bring forth children; Yet your desire will be for your husband, And he will rule over you." —Genesis 3:16 (NASB)

As we have seen, scholars indicate that women were held in very low regard during those many early centuries before Christ, making it easy to cast blame on them—as people are prone to do on perceived minority populations. Unfortunately, we are still guilty of that today! The Old Testament Book of Leviticus, however, is especially harsh on women, as we will examine, and many modern readers will no doubt feel that some of its passages are outrageous. We must bear in mind that such attitudes were supported by the culture of the time.

Hebrew culture reflected their interpretation of the Old Testament, indicating that physical pain and subjugation of women to their husbands were the direct results of Eve's transgression in the Garden. Leviticus 15:19–33 further elaborates on the plight of women and their characterization as "unclean" during times of bleeding. The Hebrew term "Niddah" refers to a woman while she is menstruating or has menstruated without finishing expected ritual requirements. Literally, the term means "separation" with the general meaning of separation from ritual impurity. A practicing Jew in the Orthodox community was expected to avoid all sexual contact with a woman in niddah. In addition to the sexual prohibition, women were even more isolated in earlier times according to Hebrew Law. Although it is not

clear why blood supposedly defiles, women during the time of bleeding that
follows childbirth were also considered unclean. Leviticus 12:1–8 specifically discusses the "Uncleanness of Childbirth," indicating two protocols for
women delivering babies. A woman delivering a boy was considered unclean
for *one* week following the birth and needed thirty-three additional days to
become purified; a woman delivering a girl, however, was considered unclean
for *two* weeks and needed sixty-six additional days to become purified. One
could only speculate about the obvious discrepancy. That point aside, formal
purification rites were required to allow women back into public interaction,
as mere contact with a menstrous woman could have dire consequences and
was the basis for many superstitions. The Hebrew law proclaiming that blood
is unclean and defiling is especially perplexing since Leviticus 17:11–14
(NAB) describes blood as "sacred" and the "seat of life," an apparent contradiction.

In addition to the physical suffering and segregation, the subjugation of
women resulted in lack of independence along with the symbols of subservience. A woman was considered the property of first her father, then her husband. In Exodus 20:17 (NASB) we observe the familiar commandment: "You
shall not covet your neighbor's house; you shall not covet your neighbor's
wife or his male servant or his female servant or his ox or his donkey or
anything that belongs to your neighbor." What contemporary people fail to
note is that this whole commandment refers to possessions. Male and female
servants were slaves, not hired help, and women were placed in the category
of possessions. In Exodus 21:2–4, a male slave owner could give a woman
as a wife to a male slave with no evidence of female agreement. The male
slave could leave after six years, but his wife and any children remained the
property of the owner. Furthermore, Exodus 21:7 allows a father to sell his
daughter as a slave and although a male slave would be freed after six years,
a female slave remained a slave indefinitely. She would not be indulged the
right to express an opinion in public and would dutifully cover her head,
symbolic of her subservience to men (Pagels; Johnson). A woman had very
little control over her own destiny in the Judaic culture of the time.

Jesus demonstrated different behaviors towards women, despite his
Hebrew heritage. He treated them as equals, often traveling in their company.
Some of his closest female companions emerged as leaders of the Church,

only to be later disavowed by misogynists. Jesus mentions the Fall only once in the New Testament, and that reference was intended as defense of marriage and protection for women (Matthew 19:4–6).

A Hebrew man could "take a wife," as they called it, and later divorce her for failure to produce an heir or for any frivolous reason he considered an "indecency" (Deuteronomy 24:1). (Women were not allowed to divorce for any reason!) The estranged husband was only required to write a note indicating the indecency. At a time of high illiteracy, writing a note may have helped reduce but not eliminate hasty divorce decisions. When Jesus argues that "indecency" should be limited to adultery and that the sanctity of marriage should otherwise remain intact (Matthew 19:9), he is attempting to equalize the field for men and women. As in any controversial change of status, misogynists would again employ their own interpretations and twist the basis of Jesus' intent.

Since we have mentioned misogyny so often, perhaps we need to briefly examine its meaning. Misogyny has existed for at least three thousand years and the word derives from two Greek words, "misein" (to hate) and "gyne" (woman). Disdain for women is evident in the Greek philosophies of Plato (ca. 427–347 BCE) and Aristotle (384–322 BCE), along with multiple references to the lower status of women in the Old Testament originating approximately 3300 years ago. Bias against women was continued into the New Testament as evidenced in numerous readings including 1 Corinthians 11:3 "the head of a woman is her husband" (RSV) and 1 Timothy 2:9–15 cautioning women against wearing fancy clothes, warning them to be silent and subordinate to their husbands. Those who gave misogynistic slants to Jesus' words and actions undermined the doctrines of love he espoused.

Considering all the information above, it appears that belief in a myth as truth rather than as metaphor was the basis for both conscious and subconscious degradation of all females and emerged as the underpinning of sexism.

Interpreting the Metaphor

Joseph Campbell discusses the story of the Fall as metaphor. "Metaphor," he says, "is an image that suggests something else. When you call someone a 'nut,' you don't mean the person is really a nut. The reference of a metaphor in religious tradition is to something transcendent that is not literally anything. If you think the metaphor is itself the reference, it would be like going to a restaurant, asking for the menu, seeing beefsteak written there and then starting to eat the menu." Campbell asserts that all religions have their legitimate truths as long as they are viewed metaphorically. Religions run into trouble, however, when they interpret metaphors as facts.

Christianity evolved out of Judaism as a "defiant sect," as it is often called. In the early days following the Crucifixion, celebrating the faith was usually done in private homes, even in kitchens. Women played an integral role, including baking the bread critical to the consecration. The home was inviting, welcoming, and inclusive, employing simple rituals. As the fledgling religion caught on and expanded, however, worship was moved to more formal institutions. Women then played a lesser role, more and more rules were established and enforced, and a top-down hierarchy prevailed.

As metaphor, the homes were inclusive and open whereas the formal churches were intimidating, structured, and uninviting, but inspiring awe. Sadly, the farther removed the Church became from the life of Christ, the more restrictive and dogmatic it became. Politics of the times drove a multitude of changes.

The discovery of the Gnostic Gospels in 1945 and their subsequent translations and interpretation brought to light the lack of unity and consensus among early Christian thinkers and theologians. Controversy and information-convolution prevailed during the first three centuries as many Christian groups, subgroups, and sects argued on behalf of their views of Christian doctrine. The fourth and fifth centuries were equally chaotic as radical and liberal ideas clashed. Heresy was born and deviation from the dogma would not be tolerated. Death was often the price of deviation from orthodox views.

Constantine's conversion to Christianity in 313 CE was instrumental in its proliferation. Establishing a policy of tolerance towards Christianity and ultimately helping to make it the official religion of the Roman Empire, Constantine exposed what had been just another Jewish sect to an expansive population and removed the fear of persecution of the faithful. There is some speculation regarding the true motivation for Constantine's conversion, but he did manage to retrofit the Christian religion into the customs, pomp, and politics of imperial Rome. This accommodation had an impact on the calendar, holidays, and celebrations, as well as an apparent influence on liturgy and ceremonies.

Some may be surprised to learn that there is no evidence that December 25 was the official birthday of Jesus. Although the actual date had been forgotten, early Christians wanted to celebrate his birth and it is probable that Constantine provided them with that date. The Roman emperor had long been a sun worshipper, a religion associated with Isis, who was often depicted as a Madonna nursing a holy infant. December 25 was the sun's "birthday" following the winter solstice and *Sun*day was proclaimed the day of rest. Such adaptation of familiar dates and customs paved the way for pagans to accept this new "state religion."

Other pagans felt admiration for the Christian value and practice of love and charity towards everyone. Pagan women were especially attracted to Christianity in the early days when Christian women were given certain privileges in keeping with Jesus' example. For a time they were considered equals to men and marriage vows were considered binding for both genders. But the status of women would all change in a short time as a result of changing Church doctrine.

Constantine also made structural changes to the Christian hierarchy. Having served as Pontifex Maximus, high priest, to the gods prior to his conversion, the emperor considered himself a bishop in the Christian Church. A Pontifex Maximus presided over state ceremonies, oversaw the calendar, and could select vestal virgins and priests. Retrofitting the format of the Christian Church into the structure of imperial Rome seemed logical and appropriate to him. He was, after all, the emperor, and a convert.

Constantine was the first to refer to bishops and priests as "clerical" and "clerics." He created a separate and exclusive clerical class, which was accorded the same rights and privileges formerly applied to pagan priests and vestal virgins. Then significantly in the fourth century, Constantine effected a State Church by blending religion and imperial politics, and the Roman State could no longer be viewed as the enemy by Christians. The former persecutors had become partners and Christianity was "re-formed" to better meet the needs of a Church-State. We can be wary and critical of some of

Constantine's actions, but we also have to wonder if Christianity would have survived without its inclusion in the Roman culture and practice and if so, what form might it have taken?

Original Sin and Sex

Today, just the *word* "sex" usually captures people's attention and imagination; but early Christians were more preoccupied with *Parousia*, the Second Coming, than they were with sex and rules for reproduction. Expecting Christ's return, they considered the Final Judgment imminent. As decades passed and Parousia did not happen, however propagation again became a necessary objective.

With the exception of Jesus' reference to the sanctity of marriage, neither Jesus nor Paul specifically mentioned sex. Celibacy was praised as a virtue but not a requirement in the New Testament, and the need to propagate had been emphasized in the Old Testament. The Church struggled to reconcile the pursuit of celibacy with the need for propagation through marriage and often was unclear in its statements on sex. The choice of celibacy was "best," but the choice of marriage was acceptable. In early Christianity priests could be married, although some felt marriage was incompatible with the duties of a cleric. It fell to Augustine (354–430), Bishop of Hippo from 396–430, to put sex on the map, so to speak.

Augustine of Hippo

Sin is usually defined as a transgression against God, causing an estrangement between the sinner and God. During the first four centuries of the Common Era, the first (Original) "sin" was considered to be the disobedience of Adam and Eve. By the end of the fourth century, however, that doctrine changed. The "sin" came to be viewed in a different manner, thanks in great measure to Augustine's interpretation of the Genesis creation story. He concluded that sexual desire is sinful, that infants are infected with Original Sin at the time of conception, and that Adam's sin corrupted even nature itself. Surely involuntary erections are physical proof, according to Augustine, of the innate evil of sex.

In her book *Adam, Eve, and the Serpent,* Elaine Pagels discusses her translation of Augustine's spin on the Genesis creation story in which he claims that Adam and Eve's actions cost more than our mortality. He says it cost us our moral freedom bestowed by God before the Fall, permanently corrupted our sexual experiences, and disavowed human claim to genuine political freedom. Pagels asserts that such views played very well into the politics of the evolving Church-State and established the need for governing the populace. It seems apparent that Augustine had carried the condemnation of sexuality and its ramifications much further than most of his contemporary Christians and Jews.

Augustine of Hippo, later elevated to sainthood, has been hailed as one of the greatest Christian teachers and leaders. What could have caused him to view life in such a dark and negative fashion? Examining some characteristics and events of his life provides clues.

As a young man, Augustine had a classical Latin education and studied Roman rhetoric, including expressive and persuasive speech. Although he was known for his extensive sexual adventures, one of which provided him with a son, Augustine became associated with Manichaeism.

Manichaeism was the teaching of a group whose beliefs were based on the concept of the duality of light and darkness. Light was associated with knowledge, spirit, and soul while darkness was associated with ignorance, matter, and body. Believers found redemption through "moral" practices such as abstinence from sex, wine, and meat.

The duality of Manichaeism provided Augustine with excuses for his own behavior. He rationalized that he could not be held accountable for his own actions and failures if life were innately evil. Nonetheless, exposure to other philosophies and ideas caused him consternation as he struggled to reconcile contradictory concepts with his sexual appetite. Reading Cicero's *Hortensius,* for example, Augustine was particularly struck by the concept that sensual pleasures are incompatible with discipline of thought. Similar philosophies affected him in the same way, as he agonized over his lifestyle and lack of discipline.

Augustine faced a real conflict of interest after years of satisfying his sexual appetite while searching for intellectual and spiritual answers. His mother Monica's prayers at last were answered when he finally embraced

Christianity during his thirties. The monastic model of Saint Anthony and his followers, who gave up all earthly possessions and pleasures, as well as some meaningful words of Saint Paul, provided the final inspiration for Augustine's conversion.

Although he served in the monastic life for several years, much to his chagrin Augustine became an instant priest in 391 at the urging of Bishop Valerius in Hippo. His rhetorical skills were so impressive that he became Bishop of Hippo just five years later. His past experiences drove his opinions and informed new passions that dramatically impacted the future Church. Just as a chain smoker who quits can come to despise all smokers and smoking, Augustine condemned all pleasures of the flesh outside and inside of marriage. His view of life in general was pessimistic indeed, offering little hope of redemption for a humanity incapable of making decisions without assistance from Church and State.

Augustine used his persuasive powers and some say "bribery" to sway the decision-makers in the Church hierarchy, playing into the evolving politics of the day. A Church-State could be convinced of the need to act as guardians of an audience eager to find redemption. Such changes in doctrine caused ramifications still felt today, even by those outside the Judeo-Christian cultures.

Thomas Aquinas

As influential as Augustine was in informing Church doctrine, an even more influential figure emerged during the thirteenth century. Thomas Aquinas (1224–1274) was a brilliant scholar, theologian, and architect of Catholic orthodoxy. He was born to a family of nobility in Italy and started his studies at the University of Naples at a time (about 1236) when universities were beginning to replace monasteries as centers of culture. It was in Naples that Aquinas studied a new translation of the philosophy of Aristotle which had recently reemerged—although Aristotle's work was a forbidden topic in most universities at the time (John Wijngaards, *National Catholic Reporter,* January 14, 2000; see http://www.womenpriests.org/wijngaards/aquinas.asp). He later joined the Dominican Order despite family protestations, and in 1244 or 1245 was sent to Cologne to study with Albertus Magnus (Albert the Great), the most renowned professor of the order, who became a lifelong mentor for him. Aquinas subsequently completed his formal studies at the University of Paris.

Thomas was often referred to as "dumb ox," an unflattering nickname created no doubt because of his corpulent size and quiet, refined manner. As a young girl I remember a CCD priest sharing a legend claiming that arcs were carved out of tables to accommodate Thomas' girth! He is more appropriately remembered, however, as the greatest theologian of the Catholic Church and as one of thirty-three Doctors of the Church, an honor conferred for eminence in theology and holiness. This posthumous honor was conferred in 1567, although Thomas Aquinas had already been canonized in 1323 by Pope John XXII in Avignon.

Augustine and Aquinas on Original Sin

Augustine authored the concept of "Original Sin," and Thomas Aquinas supported it with some modifications. Augustine felt that man was originally mortal but would have earned immortality eventually had Adam and Eve not committed Original Sin. After Original Sin, man was merely mortal and was destined to die.

In contrast, in *Summa Theologica,* Aquinas described the time before the Fall as a "state of original justice" in which immortality was a gift from God. As long as original justice remained, original immortality would exist. Aquinas asserted that man was immortal before sin. After Original Sin, however, man became subject to death, which was a consequence of that transgression.

Aquinas on Sex

As noted earlier, Augustine condemned sexual passion as an evil responsible for man's expulsion from Eden. He acknowledged that Adam and Eve might have eventually formed a sexual union as a result of God's command to "Go forth and multiply," but would have done so out of will and responsiveness to God, not out of passion. He condemned sexual pleasure, which was intrinsically evil according to his philosophy.

Aquinas, on the other hand, felt that God had a plan, which was our moral duty to follow. In his wisdom, God designed sexual pleasure as an incentive and reward for procreation. Aquinas held that sexuality and sexual pleasure were permissible *only* in a monogamous marriage as part of active procreation. He went on to describe two forms of lecherous sins. First, it was a violation of God's design to perform unnatural sexual acts in which procreation could not occur and in which pleasure was sought for its own sake. Second, sexual activities having procreative potential but violating acceptable relations in society were usually considered venial sins. Examples included rape, incest, adultery by a married man, and seducing a virgin still living in her father's house. It is interesting to note that Aquinas extended procreation to include responsibility for a child into adulthood.

Aquinas on Women

Although Aquinas does not seem to have been as blatantly misogynistic as Augustine, his views also dealt a negative blow to women. His opinions were based partially on adhering to Aristotelian views and partly on misinformation regarding human biology held as truth until the 1800s.

Men were believed to hold the seed of life that was to be injected into the wombs of women, who were merely receptacles and nurturers until the child was born. The Greco-Roman view of procreation claimed that there was only one gender in two forms. Insufficient "heat" or "vital spirit" in early gestation resulted in the birth of a woman. Based on this view, Thomas reasoned that females were incomplete males, "deficient and unintentionally caused."

He further reasoned that women possess inferior intellectual powers and do not reflect the image of God. Furthermore, in keeping with Aristotelian philosophy that the soul is part of the body, Thomas deduced that the female soul is also inferior, raising questions about redemption.

We should underscore the fact that Thomas Aquinas was a renowned scholar, however, who taught that theology must prove what it teaches. As an acknowledged truth-seeker he surely would agree today to recant his own fifteenth-century teachings, given the discovery of the ovum in 1827 and our more accurate scientific understanding of biology today.

Conclusion

With Original Sin firmly established as Christian doctrine and Baptism the prescribed remedy, the presumably "blemished" nature of mankind necessitated the related doctrines of hell and heaven, purgatory and limbo. If people were prone to sin, how might they earn redemption? Penance was required to achieve a "state of grace." "Indulgences," though controversial, also were devised as a means to achieve that "state of grace."

Even the relatively optimistic Aquinas felt that the chances of redemption and reaching heaven were remote for some and unlikely or impossible for most. We may conclude that in great measure fear had replaced love as the prime motivation for behavior in Christianity by Aquinas' time. This root of practice has been modified somewhat through subsequent centuries, but not until after great harm had already been done to the western psyche and its consciousness. Guilt became part of our cellular memory, along with a growing conviction that Eve is the cause of life's misery and our ultimate death.

2

Spinning the Yarn

In the previous chapter we learned that Christianity evolved from a small sect of passionate followers of Jesus to a mega-church-state hierarchical structure. We played with the Fall from Eden story and showed how adhering to it as historical fact provided a rationale for misogyny. We understand that many early followers of Jesus gave their own meaning to their Master's life, resurrection, and message, and that struggles for consistency and clarity in the fledgling religion ensued.

Although many battled for their positions, three key figures changed the course of Christianity. Each applied his individual spins to effect key changes in direction. In the fourth century, Constantine and Rome consolidated and retrofitted the contending groups—first by selecting the "truth" and then by proliferating that tweaked message throughout the Roman Empire. During the fourth and fifth centuries, Augustine of Hippo provided a dismal portrayal of the human plight by establishing Original Sin, mankind's evil nature, and the need for repentance as a foundation of Christianity. Eve and her temptress sisters and sex had caused the downfall. The great scholar Thomas Aquinas substantiated much of Augustine's premise in the thirteenth century, holding out hope for redemption to an elite and holy few.

How were these three men so successful in winning over the opposition and their differing views? Why were so many people willing to accept church/state decisions and some might say harsh rules and restrictions? The spin given to the myth of the Fall gave ammunition to Augustine, Aquinas, and others to hold sex as evil; but for what reasons might women find celibacy attractive, given the status of their lives? Fear was surely one motivator they used for behavior modification; they also used clever persuasion and "spin" to bring church leaders and public opinion to their way of thinking.

Defining the Spin

We are familiar with the term "spin" in today's society, seeing it daily in the media and online. We recognize it as an interpretation of a particular action by a group or individual with vested interests to serve or protect. Similarly to the perspective one takes with respect to a glass being half empty or half full, some people use this tactic as a political ploy to advance their view in the best light. "Spinning" may also be used as skillful tool for manipulation or as an effort to save face.

What is the derivation and significance of the concept of spin? Consider the backstory:

"Spin," as commonly used in today's vernacular, probably traces from the expression "spinning the yarn." The meanings and usages of both "spin" and "yarn" evolved separately over time and vary in connotation according to context and agenda. Derivation of the phrase and the individual words, however, has a direct relationship to the communication of information.

I first heard the expression when I was a young child, watching an old-fashioned Western movie. Gabby Hayes, a cantankerous old cowpoke, sat around the campfire cooking "grub" and telling "yarns" —tall tales about his most recent escapades. A generic definition of a "yarn" was usually an oral story repeated many times and intended as entertainment. And just as fish tales tend to be greatly exaggerated, yarns had the same reputation for embellishment.

There are multiple explanations for the origin of the phrase. Some say it derives from women spinning yarn on a spinning wheel. A similar reference associates "spinning yarns" with early family projects, working together in the process of making clothing. Combing fibers, twisting them into thread, dying and weaving them into cloth, cutting the cloth and sewing it into clothing required the team effort of several people working closely together.

Since the process of spinning was a rote task, however, it provided a perfect opportunity to tell stories which may have become "tweaked" over time. It had the effect of the telephone game played at children's parties in which the original message gets distorted and changed after multiple tellings, mishearings, and misunderstandings. It is a simple leap to picture putting together threads of information in a particular manner for use in weaving the fabric of a story.

Others insist, however, that the expression has its roots in nautical lore. Sailors would literally spin or loosely twist yarns of old ropes for future use in small tasks. They would typically twist the yarns on rainy days in a sheltered area, setting the scene for story-telling and perhaps some "fish tales" (Beavis & McClosky, *Salty Dog Talk: The Nautical Origins of Everyday Expressions*).

When someone spins fibers they need to constantly stretch the material, adjusting it to maintain the necessary shape and twist. Metaphorically speaking, stretching the truth had a similar meaning to spinning a yarn.

Let's also factor in the spider spinning a web, often a metaphor for creating a complicated pattern to attract and entrap unsuspecting insects

The term "spin doctor" did not emerge until the 1980s. It was a term for "someone employed to promote, and usually masterful at concocting, positive interpretations of negative news" (http://www.word-detective.com/072104. html). Following the Reagan/Mondale debate, a *New York Times* story on October, 21, 1984, reported "A dozen men in good suits and women in silk dresses will circulate smoothly among reporters, spouting confident opinions. They won't be just press agents trying to impart a favorable spin to a routine press release. They'll be the Spin Doctors . . ." According to the July 21, 2004, issue of *Word Detective*, the first use of "doctor" with "spin" was probably intended to evoke the late-eighteenth-century connotation of "to disguise, falsify, or tamper with" as in the phrase "doctor the books."

My task in this book is to apply this meaning of "spin" to actions and events that transpired in the course of Christianity's evolution and, in the process, expose the truth about Christianity's conscious and subconscious subjugation of women and the marginalization of its female leaders. I contend that some early Church leaders practiced the art of spin as a form of persuasion, sometimes exploiting fear to motivate an illiterate, unsophisticated laity. Myths served to explain the unknown.

Early Christians were filled with the joy of imminent *Parousia* and reunion with their master. Freed from the sin of Adam and Eve by baptism and the sacrifice of Jesus, people seemed eager to purify themselves with fasting and celibacy. Procreation was irrelevant at that point. But as we noted, when *Parousia* did not come, Christians settled back into normalcy.

Constantine was emperor of Rome and through his power and authority could proclaim Christianity the official church of the state. Non-Christians had to obey, but were appeased by his retrofitting of Christianity into their past practices. Careful thought might indicate, however, that those who initially chose Christianity might be more devoted to its core principles than those who were Christians by mandate.

Although Augustine's doctrines prevailed, it is important to be aware that there were many challengers to his rhetoric. Pelagius, for example, was a major challenger who was convincing to many. Both he and Augustine used Genesis 1–3 as a basis for their reasoning, but they came to vastly different conclusions through a method called religious deduction (Pagels, *Adam, Eve, and the Serpent*, p. 130). The scientific model familiar to us was apparently not held in high esteem at the time.

Pelagius, a Celtic monk (ca. 354–418), vehemently disagreed with Augustine's assertion that man is innately evil and that God has preordained that an outside entity should dominate the masses that are presumed incapable of making decisions for themselves. Pelagius argued that Adam's sin hurt only him and was not transmitted to all mankind. He also disagreed with Augustine's premise that man can gain salvation only through the Church. He strongly believed in free will and the basic goodness of humans.

But by that time bishops were familiar with using both ecclesiastical censure and strategies influencing imperial power to make their points and get their way. It was reported that in the process of wooing the emperor's support, African Bishop Alypius, a close associate and colleague of Augustine, actually brought eighty Numidian stallions to the court as a bribe to influence the imperial court against Pelagius (Pagels, p. 129). In this case, bribery and spin helped persuade the influential figures, and Pelagius was ultimately condemned as a heretic. History cites him as one who attempted to dispute the doctrine of Original Sin.

As we learned earlier, there were many differing opinions and dissenters who met similar fates as heretics. Heretics were excommunicated, sometimes tortured or even killed, and certainly sentenced to lose salvation for eternity! Augustine convinced western Catholic and Protestant theologians to agree with him, perhaps to further bolster the sacrifice of Christ for the sins of man. The interpretation given to the doctrine of the Fall also validated the need for interdependence of church and state. Church and state authorities needed little convincing after Augustine's spin established the need for people to be governed.

But what about the common folk? Through the direct teachings and sacrifice of Jesus, freedom had become part of the underpinnings of early Christianity. Prior to the time of Constantine, Christians were persecuted and understandably considered the "state" to be their enemy. "Freedom" from Roman rule and oppression was considered a precious commodity.

"Libertas" to Romans meant "living under the rule of a good governor, an emperor of whom the Senate approved" (Pagels, p. 119). To early Christians, this state of affairs was closer to their enslavement than to freedom. After Constantine's conversion and Christianity's establishment as the official "state religion," however, they could not use the same argument. Augustine's assertion that human beings can't be trusted to govern themselves because of the corruption of nature is not conducive to freedom as many might define it. Others described it as "freedom from superior authority and from constraint" (Pagels, p. 119).

Falling into line in lockstep fashion to avoid the horrors of Hell can hardly be called freedom in any sense. But they did fall into line.

Celibacy

The introduction of celibacy into Christianity was at first viewed by many women as a chance for freedom, although that sounds paradoxical. Females could choose celibacy over arranged marriages and subjugation to husbands. Restraint from sex prevented potential pregnancies as well as the pain of childbearing and the responsibilities that follow. Although celibacy was indeed a form of restraint, it was a vehicle to gain control over one's own life. In today's society, eating disorders are frequently blamed on a female's attempt to gain control over something in her life. Control over food intake through purging helps the woman gain a perceived control over her body. It's a matter of perspective.

Women were expected to marry around the time of puberty; but as Christian laws began to impact women's property rights, some women of nobility chose a single life to avoid the usurping of their wealth and property by husbands. This resulted in a convent of noble ladies where culture and education were encouraged and fostered. Such abbeys became very powerful. According to a seventh-century papal bull, the Virgin House of the Blessed Marys and Holy Doves and Kindly Ones was proclaimed free from taxation and episcopal jurisdiction and remained free from episcopal jurisdiction until 1874 (Walker, *The Woman's Encyclopedia of Myths and Secrets*, p. 176). Abbesses were powerful and could license bishops and priests within their own districts, nominate ecclesiastical judges, hear criminal cases, and establish new parishes. This was one arena in which women were able to experience freedom and opportunity, but it was essentially for women of means. Ordinary citizens could not afford such choices.

In a controversial book researched for twenty years and published in 1893, American feminist Matilda Joslyn Gage devotes an explosive chapter to celibacy in Christianity. In light of the notoriety of current issues of sexual abuse by clergy of young boys in particular, it is especially intriguing that she was writing about this allegation more than a hundred years ago. Because of her assertions, her book *Woman, Church and State* was banned in this country and Gage herself was written out of her role in history as a leader in the Women's Suffrage Movement. The Women's Suffrage Group had joined forces with the Women's Christian Temperance League to broaden their base and increase their chances for success in achieving voting rights. In the view of many in both groups, Gage's strong opposition to blending church and state might thwart their efforts to achieve voting rights for women and jeopardize the whole suffrage movement.

Gage blames some of the sexual abuses of her time on the requirement for celibacy among priests, along with banning marriage, which was finally achieved by the Fourth Lateran Council in 1215 under the papacy of Pope Innocent III. Although the First Nicene Council had made a pronouncement in 325 against mandatory celibacy, the issue was a hot topic for many centuries. Gage claims that celibacy was difficult to enforce, so the Church felt compelled to take a number of actions, but not without unfortunate consequences including:

- Reinforcement of the doctrine of women's inherent evil
- Control of civil law by Canon Law
- An "organized system of debauchery . . . under the mask of priestly infallibility"
- Auricular confession confirmed as Church dogma
- Enforcement of prohibiting scriptures to laity
- System of indulgences strengthened, providing increased revenue to Church
- Broader parameters for heresy with more severe punishments
- Establishment of Inquisition
- Unfair punishment of families of married priests.

The decision to ban marriage for priests was supposedly based on the premise that clerics could not attend to their religious duties if they were burdened by the responsibilities due a wife and family. Contemporary Rabbi Shmuley Boteach disagrees by pointing out that married religious leaders are better able to deal with the issues of families in their charge. In an online article I originally found in the *New Jersey Jewish News* entitled "The Catholic Church and the High Price of Celibacy" (now at http://www.something jewish.co.uk/articles/1442_the_new_pope.htm), Boteach claims, "Religion is above all about family." He asserts that married clerics and their families who socialize with parish families promote greater normalcy and empathy and decrease the incidence of abuse and lack of understanding of real family issues.

Rabbi Boteach poses some provocative questions, including the challenge of creating a society in which women are respected by men if the message conveyed is that the men who run the Church do so better without a woman.

He goes on to question the validity of a priest teaching his flock that sexuality can be sanctified and that love is holy when the priest must "remove himself from the possibility of corruption from a physical relationship." What is the message sent to young people? Rabbi Boteach asks Pope Benedict XVI to take up the long argued issue of "sacerdotal marriage" and reconsider the positive impacts such a change in dogma might bring about for the Catholic Church.

Gage claims that research and records indicate a far more sinister rationale for banning marriage for priests. She states, "Although the laws against the marriage of priests were enacted on the pretense of the greater inherent weakness of women, history proves their chief object to have been keeping all priestly possessions under church control." The theme of her book constantly underscores the blatant misogynistic tendencies of blaming Eve for the woes of man. Eve's great sin in their minds justifies female subservience to males, women's imperfect state, and even the questionable status of their souls for a time.

Priests who were married at the time of the edict in the twelfth century, she tells us, were required to abandon their wives and children. Those who refused to comply were at first denied the rights of their office, and then were threatened with excommunication. Excommunication was quickly reversed if the priest finally came around and renounced his wife and family. Those who stubbornly refused compliance were denied Christian burial, which at the time was synonymous with condemnation to hell for eternity. At the time of the priests' death, real estate and other valuables left to their families were confiscated. Wives were denied the Eucharist and were labeled as harlots and the children bastards. Those families who still failed to cooperate were shunned and could be punished further or even sold as slaves for the Church's benefit. Such actions were defended since the woman reputedly stood between her husband and God and therefore must be in league with Satan (Gage, p. 82).

Priests who complied with the Church requirement may have abandoned their families, but they were not expected to abstain from sex. The Church actually encouraged priests to take mistresses, charging a mandatory concubine tax to each priest to support local "houses of vile character." Gage

(p. 94) says that parishioners often compelled priests to do so to protect their own wives and daughters!

Somehow, according to Gage, a topsy-turvy practice emerged—one in which chastity was associated with employment of concubines and "unchastity" was associated with marriage. She again attributes that opinion to holding women responsible for the Fall which Church Fathers argued necessitated the institution of marriage. Women were considered impure and appropriately subservient; priests were considered to be infallible during the Middle Ages. Immorality with a priest was supposedly a holy act, giving the woman a "claim to heaven." Thus the Church supported the chastity of concubinage and the unchastity of marriage, according to Gage.

Talk about spin! Twisting information to justify illogical conclusions.

Heaven and Hell

In the daily life of the populace, the mystery of the origins of life and what happens after death is both puzzling and frightening. People in pain are relieved to finally have a diagnosis, as long as the treatment provides hope for a cure. Fear of the unknown is the worst, but fear itself is often the major motivator in behavioral change.

Unfortunately, some fanatic religious leaders took advantage of this common element in human nature and used fear tactics to feed their own need for power, control, and wealth. Many of their tactics spun teachings about Heaven and Hell to sell the idea that people need the Church to get into the first and to escape the otherwise certain horrors of the other. Their convincing propaganda initiated a strange symbiotic relationship: the Church needed blind acceptance from the populace to wield power, and the populace believed they needed the Church to find salvation. To be saved from the pangs of hellfire and damnation, all Christians were expected to strictly obey the rules; but women seemed to bear the heavier shackles, chaining them with these powerful threats to narrowly defined roles.

As early Christians struggled to determine the cause of their misery, pain, and death, for women and men alike it was almost a relief to find someone to blame and share the guilt. People were willing to believe the Church's teaching that they were inherently evil and aspire to abide by the dictates of a learned and wise clerical hierarchy—if it would serve them to do so. In a sense, they were brainwashed as a child might be upon hearing day after day that he or she is ugly or stupid or lazy. One tends to believe it. They could accept responsibility as long as the Church in its turn provided them with the tools for salvation. Strict adherence to the rules and completing difficult penance requirements would put them on the path towards heaven. Deals could be made.

Some of the deals, though—as we'll see in this chapter and others—were unbelievably dirty for women from the perspective we enjoy today.

Attributing suffering to sin—as was done by rabbis, shamans, and Augustinian theory—was a form of "social control," according to Elaine Pagels: "As long as people are willing to accept blame for events outside their control, the religious elite can manipulate a gullible majority into following otherwise unacceptable discipline" (p. 146). Pagels also speculates that Augustinian theory actually filled a need for those who would rather feel guilty than helpless. She further postulates that, without the willingness of the populace to accept guilt, the concept of Original Sin might not have survived the fifth century. Instead it became the foundation for Christian teachings for sixteen hundred years.

In the afterlife, according to classical mythology, departing souls called shades of the dead went to Hades, a mysterious and dark place. Persian Zoroastrian priests actually developed the concept of physical hell that was later adopted by the Jews and Christians. It was the Christians who creatively described the torments of Hell, however, and proclaimed that the torture would go on forever.

Although many were originally attracted to Christianity because of its promise of salvation, some early Church Fathers insisted that the threat of Hell helped justify the existence of Heaven (Johnson, p. 231). The reward for baptism followed by good life as defined by the Church resulted in a place in Heaven and eternal happiness. Failure to live as prescribed would result in failure to achieve such bliss, but descriptions of the heavenly condition were vague. Later artists' renditions would portray images of what Heaven might look like; but at a time when the earth was considered flat, it was easy to depict Heaven as up in the clouds and Hell as down below. Volcanic fire from the belly of the earth provided artists and theologians with horrific images of the characteristics of Hell. Descriptions of Hell were for centuries far more vivid than descriptions of Heaven!

John Scotus Erigena, a ninth-century Irishman, was the only Christian to deny the existence of Hell as it was described from the time of Augustine until the Reformation. He vehemently rejected the existence of a material, eternal place of horrific punishment and torture, claiming that one's "pangs of conscience" would cause pain and anxiety; but he disapproved of sharing that concept pastorally. Some theologians subscribed to a "double truth"—that is, expressing their honest opinion in private, yet creating the full horrific descriptions for the laity. And create they did! (Johnson, pp. 341–42)

Theologians described Hell most passionately, employing images so graphic you'd be convinced they had been there. Augustine, Peter Lombard, and Aquinas—giants among medieval teachers—all subscribed to the doctrine that Hell was a fiery physical place with spiritual aspects as well. Writers seemed to take delight in using "Hollywood-like" descriptions to scare the "bejeebers" out of all those sinners!

Jerome (ca. 340–420), a Doctor of the Church, claimed that Hell was like a huge winepress. German writers and artists carried this metaphor further, claiming that a hundred million damned souls would be squeezed into every square mile of Hell and would be treated like grapes in a winepress, bricks in a furnace, salt sediment in a barrel of pickled fish, and sheep in a slaughterhouse (Johnson, p. 341).

Augustine described Hell as peopled by ferocious flesh-eating animals which tore humans to bits slowly and painfully, though they themselves were immune to the flames (Johnson, p.341). Richard Rolle's colorful description of Hell in "Stimulus Conscientiae" claimed that the condemned tear and eat their own flesh, drink the gall of dragons and the venom of asps, and suck the heads of adders, and that their bedding and clothing consisted of horrible venomous vermin.

The French focused instead on psychological pain, citing that when the damned asked about the time, the response was eternity. Hell has no clocks, only an eternal ticking (Johnson, p. 341).

Most Christian writers also espoused that the pain of loss and separation was part of the psychological consequence. Aquinas added that part of the pleasure of Heaven was observing the sufferings of the damned, a sentiment shared and defended by both Calvinists and Catholics. So much for the compassionate conservatism of the time!

Catholics were taught that those who denied the existence of Hell were headed there. Even Luther supported the concept of Hell, and orthodox belief in Hell is indicated in the Lutheran Augsburg Confession (1530) article 17 (Johnson, p. 341).

By the eighteenth century, new scientific knowledge helped to modify the visions of Hell. Despite the effectiveness of using the threat of Hell as a deterrent to sin, it became more difficult to reconcile a loving God with the ferocious punishments. Hell remains, nonetheless, part of the doctrine of some Christian sects to this day.

Between Heaven and Hell

According to Church teachings, few believers would get to Heaven and most would find themselves in Hell for their unholy behaviors and shortcomings. The concept of Purgatory, however, offered a compromise and hope. Why would people continue to follow rules if there were no hope for redemption? Where was the salvation promised to them since the beginnings of Christianity? What was the meaning of prayer? What purpose would priests and bishops serve? Purgatory provided the perfect answer.

The early Church Fathers actually discussed an in-between place or intermediate state on the way to Heaven. Prayers for the dead would then make sense. For those in Hell, it was too late; and for those in Heaven, prayers were not needed. But, praying to help move a soul out of a "holding place" faster gave a real purpose. Prayer could also help those on earth shorten their stay in Purgatory.

Purgatory and prayers for the dead were initiated by the Council of Carthage in 394 and were upheld by subsequent major councils. Purgatory did not become part of formal Church dogma until the sixteenth century, however. Originally described as a "dreadful place of painful, long-lasting punishment by fire," more recent descriptions refer to Purgatory as a "condition of life" rather than an actual place. The *Catholic Encyclopedia* currently describes Purgatory as "the condition or state for those who have not totally alienated themselves from God by their sins, but who are temporarily and partially alienated from God while their love is made perfect and they give satisfaction for their sins."

Martin Luther originally believed in the "undeniable existence of Purgatory," but later rejected it based on lack of evidence in biblical passages. Since 1530, all Protestant denominations have eliminated the doctrine of Purgatory; but belief in Purgatory by all Christians for many centuries drove behaviors and laid the groundwork for confession, penance, and indulgences.

Confession and Reconciliation

Baptism was originally a purification process in preparation for *Parousia*. When *Parousia* didn't come, post-baptismal sin and repentance became problematic. Priests would intercede to God for those who publicly confessed to them.

Public confession was the standard until 459, when Leo I forbade public confessions. He asserted that sinners should confess to God and then to a priest or bishop who in turn would pray for them. Gregory the Great held that confession, probably accompanied by a ceremony, was required for the remission of sin (Johnson, p. 231).

The Council of Chalons in 813 determined that confessions made in private to God were as valid as those made to priests, but the Lateran Council of 1216 finally made auricular confession compulsory for all adult Christians. Although sixteenth-century reformers denied that confession was a sacrament (Johnson, p. 231), the Council of Trent in 1545 called it divine. As significant as confession became, however, it was the penance ascribed to the sinner that established the mechanism for earning salvation. Bear in mind that once the sin has been confessed, the temporal punishment still remains. The sinner must pay for those sins either in Purgatory where sins are purged, or through indulgences.

Penance and Indulgence

The possibility of achieving salvation was dismal during the Dark Ages. Aquinas had stated that few would be saved and many would be damned;

and later medieval preachers held out hope for only one in a thousand, even one in ten thousand. Given that grim statistic, believers were willing to do whatever it took to increase their chances for being saved from the fires.

During the Dark Age, penance was felt to be compensation to an angry God for sins committed, and assignments were extremely arduous and harsh. Fasting, often accompanied by mandated pilgrimages to holy places or frequent visits to shrines, was a common penance. Johnson (p. 231) cites an example according to Wulfstan of York in which a man was sentenced to fast barefoot three days a week for the rest of his life, to wear one woolen garment, and to have only three haircuts a year! Another example cited was for a person guilty of patricide, a fairly common Dark Age crime. The penitent was exiled, bound in chains, and charged to travel on pilgrimages until his chains fell off.

One real problem with penance lay in the inconsistencies and discrepancies meted out to sinners. Customs varied from region to region, and some penances were so severe that penitents lived in constant fear of failing to complete them. (Actually, that was a major reason for adopting the theory of Purgatory.) Ironically, while public confessions were the norm, common folk felt that all were spiritually equal under God since even kings and archbishops could be required to endure brutal beatings. That practice would also change.

Another challenge emerged during the seventh century, when men began to perform other people's penance for a fee. The Church opposed such commutation, but approved "vicarious penance without pay" which was performed out of love or perhaps fear or hope for a future favor. This proved to be a loophole.

Giving alms to the poor was considered a form of penance, but the rich might take an unfair advantage of that opportunity. Through careful analysis, the Church approved the process based on some apparent biblical justification. Johnson (p. 232) credits such approval on the "probable spin of a canon lawyer for his professional purposes." Nonetheless, citing Proverbs, 13:8— "The ransom of a man's life are his riches" (KJ)—and Luke 16:9— "Make to yourselves friends of the mammon of unrighteousness; that when ye fail, they may receive you into everlasting habitations" (KJ)—the case was made for allowing rich sinners to buy their way out of harsh penance.

The rich could establish "ecclesiastical endowments," donating money to a monastery or convent in return for the monks' or nuns' prayers. As a result, "penitent" rich men funded abbeys and priories to atone for grievous sins, especially during the tenth, eleventh, and twelfth centuries.

Indulgences are merited as penance is completed through prayers or deeds and are categorized as either "plenary" or "partial." Plenary indulgences accommodate and "pay for" all existing temporal punishment owed for a person's sins. Such indulgences are limited to one per day. Partial indulgences only "pay for" part of the existing punishment.

In 1095, Urban II attempted to entice men into volunteering for the First Crusade to the holy land by offering complete remission for sins and enlistment as "substitution for all other penances incurred." Serving as a Crusader was hazardous duty, however, and carried rules and great risk. During the twelfth century, crusading was nearly the only means for getting indulgences, with a very few exceptions for the wealthy or politically connected (Johnson, p. 233). Unfortunately such exceptions opened the door to future abuses.

Innocent III in the thirteenth century extended indulgences to those who provided consulting or financial contributions. Later, Innocent IV offered indulgences for special purposes other than serving on crusades. It was only a short time before indulgences were offered for political reasons, and ultimately sinners could buy plenary indulgences on their deathbeds and enter heaven immediately if they were in a state of grace (Johnson, p. 233).

By 1517, Pope Leo X was rebuilding St. Peter's Basilica in Rome and offered indulgences for those giving alms. Johann Tetzel, who was promoting this sales pitch, was said to have quipped, "As soon as the coin in the coffer rings, the soul from Purgatory springs." This activity, the supposed purchase and sale of salvation, was perceived as abuse and set off a firestorm as Martin Luther initiated steps for the Protestant Reformation, further aided and fueled by the invention of the printing press. Then and now, technology serves to change the courses of history! The Catholic Church subsequently attempted to disavow and discredit such unscrupulous bastardization of the concept of indulgences, but retained it for the benefit of the sincere penitents and those priests and preachers who went to great lengths to ensure the need of true repentance.

During this chapter we have been discussing communication skills and strategies aimed at convincing common people to behave in a certain way. People might very well take the same information and reach different conclusions; but once the Church leaders had determined the "truth" and proclaimed it canon law, all were expected to conform to that belief. It has been proven in the last several centuries, however, that individuals "tampered with" canon law as indicated in the False Decretals. Composed between 847 and 862, supposedly in France, the forgeries were apparently made by Isadore Mercatore (perhaps a pseudonym), a well-intended canonist who was attempting to make changes he felt were necessary. By integrating the forgeries into the collection of legitimate documents, and by tampering with the texts of some of them, Isadore was able to effect the change of reforming canon law in support of bishops struggling against secular interference in diocesan affairs. This sanction allowed bishops to avoid mediation of archbishops and metropolitan officials and to interact directly with "The Holy See." Its significance, regardless of the intention or outcome, is that forgeries and tampering with documents actually happened. How many others are there of which we are still unaware?

We acknowledge that people followed Church dictates acting out of a need to be led and to learn about the mysteries of the universe, as well as acting out of fear of hellfire and damnation as they struggled to find hope of reaching Paradise. The Church accommodated that need, although not always out of altruism and faith. Greed and power were unfortunate motivators for some unscrupulous leaders. Censorship and compliance along with guilt and fear were used as mechanisms of control. For many centuries the illiterate masses unquestioningly marched to the same drum.

Apologists, both Catholic and Protestant, continue to defend the actions and words of their leaders, skillfully employing the rhetoric and logic required to "convince the populace of their validity and truth." Sounds a lot like spin, doesn't it? It also sounds a lot like defenses employed by current political strategists trying to convince "the masses" of their own sincerity and purpose.

How do you define freedom? Should we march unquestioningly to a single drum?

3

Playing the Blame Game:
Crusaders, Heretics, and Witches

During their first three centuries, Christians and Christianity struggled to sort themselves out. As time progressed, those who marched to different drums than orthodox believers were perceived as traitors, turncoats from "approved truth." Pockets of such people were portrayed by Church authorities as diseases needing to be eradicated before spreading further, at whatever cost.

Generally speaking, sects elevating the roles of women, in history and/or in current function, were discounted, summarily dismissed or obliterated. Some feared that an elevation of women in Christianity would jeopardize its acceptance and longevity, given the lowly cultural stature of women at the time. But the Christian movement, which had initially equalized the genders, changed dramatically as literalists redefined roles. Furthermore, during the fourteenth and fifteenth centuries, women observed preaching or teaching religious information were associated with heresies. Both 1 Timothy 2:11 and 1 Corinthians 14:34–35 (NAB) warned women to ". . . keep silent in the churches for they are not allowed to speak, but should be subordinate, as even the law says. But if they want to learn anything, they should ask their husbands at home. For it is improper for a woman to speak in the church."

Heresy, once defined as a wise moral "choice," by the Greeks, was no longer an option for those who wished to remain Christians on the path to salvation after Irenaeus gave it a new connotation just before the turn of the third century.

In this chapter we ask:

"What were the major heresies?"

"Who were the heretics?"

"How were heretics controlled and/or punished?"

We then draw upon this background to examine how women were easy prey for Inquisitors and witch-hunts.

It's easy to understand why in the fourth century there was a perceived need to stabilize Church doctrine, which led to choosing some traditions and theologies over others. The existence of many splinter groups, often with contradictory beliefs, threatened to diffuse the still youthful religion to the point of its demise. Despite the fact that many Christian sub-groups had co-existed for nearly three centuries, the sincere faithful feared that Jesus' message would be lost forever if steps weren't taken to immortalize what they saw as his message.

Although little was known about the actual words of Jesus, early Church leaders reconstructed them from bits and pieces of information that had been conveyed through the oral tradition. There are some, however, who believe in the existence of the Lost Gospel of Q, reputed to be a collection of sayings as remembered by followers of Jesus and recorded two decades after his death. *The Gospel of Q; All Sides to the Controversy* (www.religious tolerance.org/gosp_q.htm) indicates that Jesus is supposedly described in this text as a "charismatic teacher, a simple man filled with the spirit of God" and "also a sage, the personification of Wisdom, cast in the tradition of King Solomon."

This lost document was originally named "Quelle" for "source" by German researchers but is usually abbreviated to "Q." Inferred from analysis of texts of Matthew and Luke, discovery of this hypothetical gospel would probably be welcomed by liberal Christians and no doubt rebuked by conservatives. Nonetheless, official Gospels were selected, and words, actions, behavior, and expectations were codified into dogma in 325—with many subsequent interpretations ascribed at later synods and councils, often with political motivations and agendas as we learned earlier.

While consolidation and stability were probably necessary to preserve the religion, orthodoxy had its price in the punishment of those who deviated from the accepted and approved doctrine. Let's first investigate the origin and significance of orthodoxy and the meaning and consequences of heresy.

Orthodoxy vs. Heresy

Paul Johnson (p. 22) claims that the earliest Christian sources were not writing history but rather were conveying evangelism or theology from an oral tradition remembered, interpreted, and retold time after time. But oral "documentation" was often contradictory, rife with discrepancies that were reflected in what ultimately became the four canonical gospels. According to Johnson, even those accepted gospels had gone through several steps subjecting them to further inconsistencies. They were probably circulated in colloquial Greek, although the native language of many of the early followers was Aramaic. Difficult spiritual mysteries were conceptualized and verbalized in one language, then translated and presented in Greek, a more universal language and the language of the educated. Factor in the influence of Hebrew quotations and Hellenic concepts and it's no wonder there was underlying confusion, misinterpretation, and apparent contradiction.

Paul's authentic epistles were primary sources and expressed his opinion in a direct manner. He admittedly never "walked with Jesus" nor knew him in the same manner as those who had personal connections, so his comments about Jesus the man were limited. Johnson (p. 23) tells us that Paul was such a stickler for truth that he would only describe Jesus as "a Jew born under the law of Davidic descent, who was betrayed, crucified, buried and rose again." Jewish Christians resented Paul's perceived "monopoly on truth." After all, in their minds Paul's single credential was his vision, albeit a vision which altered his life.

It was actually at the end of the second century that Irenaeus, Bishop of Lyons, declared that the oral tradition was gone for good (Johnson, p. 23). He committed his trust to the canonical writings and set out to establish the truth. Describing his own Christian views as "orthodox" (from "ortho" meaning straight and "doxa" from thinking) as opposed to his opponents' views, Irenaeus' treatise *Against Heresies* served to discredit the perspectives of his opponents and to bring the word heresy into common use.

"Heresy" is derived from the Greek word *hairesis,* meaning a choice of beliefs or a faction of dissident believers; but determination of heresy often lacks objectivity, since it is defined from the perspective of those within an established belief system. During the Reformation, for example, Roman Catholics called Protestantism heretical while some non-Catholics considered Catholicism the "Great Apostasy." Opinion is based on the view from where you sit.

New Advent in *The Catholic Encyclopedia* cites St. Thomas' definition of heresy as "a species of infidelity in men who, having professed the faith of Christ, corrupts [sic] its dogmas." The writers describe two examples of deviating from Christianity: "refusal to believe in Christ Himself," and "restricting belief to certain points of Christ's doctrine selected and fashioned at pleasure." The first was considered the path of the infidel and "common to Pagans and Jews"; the latter was considered the path of heretics. According to this posture, true Christians must commit to the whole package, the "total sum of truths revealed in Scripture and Tradition as proposed to our belief by the Church."

Heretical beliefs may be the result of ignorance, misunderstanding, or poor judgment, according to Catholic teaching. This is referred to as material heresy. More serious heretical convictions may be motivated by "intellectual pride or exaggerated reliance on one's own insight; the illusions of religious zeal; the allurements of political or ecclesiastical power; the ties of material interests and personal status" as well as possibly "more dishonorable" motivations. It is only persistent adherence to a particular heretical tenet, however, that makes the heresy "formal."

In clarifying the difference between heresy and apostasy, the apostate is described as one who "abandons wholly the faith of Christ either by embracing Judaism, Islamism, or Paganism, or simply by falling into naturalism and complete neglect of religion" whereas "the heretic always retains faith in Christ" (www.newadvent.org/cathen/07256b.htm). There is apparently no stigma attached to those who have fleeting thoughts or questions about tenets of the faith, but it appears that for Catholic Christians, it's all or nothing to remain in good standing.

Many heretical issues were related to the nature of Jesus Christ, his relationship to God the Father, the concept of the Trinity (three persons in one

God, equal and eternal), and the mystery of the divinity yet humanity of Jesus. Those concepts were deliberated and the official doctrine was determined in 325 at the First Council of Nicea.

The First Council of Nicea established the tenets of Christian faith and official doctrine. Yet Emperor Constantine, who convened and was present at the Council, was himself open-minded about some flexibility within Christian tenets. Interestingly, Constantine, who crafted the Christian church-state, believed that all people should be Christian but had no issue with those who had different views on theological issues. He felt that "sensible Christians could disagree about doctrine in the spirit of brotherly love" (Pagels, *Beyond Belief*, p. 174). Of course Constantine had been informed by a Roman culture in which a plethora of multicultural beliefs and a pantheon of gods/goddesses were tolerated in peaceful co-existence. Christians prior to Constantine's conversion ran into difficulties because of their refusal to pay homage to the emperor and to at least "honor" deities deemed critical to Rome's welfare.

Controlling heresy became a central issue as the Church's expanding hierarchy became increasingly nervous about the numerous deviations from accepted practices. Church authorities also sought uniformity and stability, fearing that "non-orthodox practices tended to attract more attention and hostility" (Johnson, p. 71). But by 382 there were strategies for dealing with heresy, including use of confession, canon law, excommunication, and authorization of punishment by death.

Confession revealed what people really felt about Church doctrine and the established faith. Use of canon law as a welcoming umbrella was a clever ploy to root out potential heresies by including "followers of old and divergent traditions." Tenets could then be put through the process of selection and canonization ultimately destroying the documents considered to be dangerous—an ingenious form of censorship.

During the first three centuries the Church could condemn heretics and deviant groups, excommunicate them, and call them names; but aside from the strategies noted above, Christian leaders lacked the clout to impose additional punishment. We should emphasize, however, that proclaimed offenders took excommunication very seriously since it was a spiritual punishment separating them from the body of Christ. That separation would no doubt cost heretics their salvation. Although orthodoxy was established during the time of Bishop Demetrius (189–231), uniformity was still not achieved by the end of the third century.

By the fourth century, however, Christianity had become the leading religion in the Roman Empire and Ambrose, Bishop of Milan (373–397), was effective in aligning imperial authority with the orthodoxy of the Catholic Church—asserting that "non-membership in the Church" was tantamount to "disloyalty to the emperor" (Johnson, p. 104). Once again it was Augustine who provided a major premise for Church action against transgressors. As a supporter of persecution and torture, his theory provided the basis for punishment that later became the basis for the Inquisition. Augustine felt that if the state could employ such tactics for criminals, the Church was certainly justified in utilizing such punishments for far greater transgressions (Johnson, p. 116). Aquinas echoed Augustine's posture, saying that convicted heretics should not only be excommunicated but also put to death immediately upon their conviction. Aquinas softened the statement, however, praising the mercy of the Church for providing several warnings and an opportunity for conversion to accused heretics. Fear again became the driving force, nonetheless. Fear of the creeping disease of heresy became so pervasive among Church leaders that it resulted in a special "crusade" in the thirteenth century.

By the end of the fifth century, Rome had been long under barbarian attacks and finally succumbed to the assaults of marauding tribes. Feudalism reigned and Europe experienced a period of decay often referred to as the Dark Ages (ca. 476–1000). In the void that arose from lack of a stable government, the Church subsumed the major responsibilities for influence and governance. Church and government remained "intertwined."

Heresies and Heretics

Church doctrine thus had been carefully erected and heresy had been defined, although parameters of tolerance seemed to change as fear of the impacts of unorthodox and unapproved beliefs escalated.

Until 1231 it was the responsibility of bishops to discover, reveal, and put down heresy. After that time, the obligation was conferred to an Inquisition

Committee, the dreaded interrogators who were charged to extirpate, stamp out, extinguish, and crush heretical beliefs. The apparent redundancy reflects my reaction to the zeal with which the Inquisitors approached their charge. Accusations of heresy often went far beyond theology and Christology—for example, attacking creative thinkers and scientists for theories and discoveries contradicting what the Church felt to be true regarding the nature of the universe.

There were many heretics and heresies. One of the initial forms of heresy in Christianity's earliest days was Gnosticism. Derived from the Greek word "gnosis" for knowledge, believers felt salvation could be reached through hidden knowledge rather than through faith. Gnostics often believed that Christ had revealed this hidden knowledge through special instructions given to his apostles and cited New Testament verses as proof (for example, Mark 4:33–34 or 1 Corinthians 2:6–7).

Some Gnostics felt that Christ was a great prophet, but denied his divinity. Many believed in Dualism, the view of two powerful Gods in the Universe: one good and the creator of all things spiritual and heavenly; the other "evil," often associated with the Old Testament, creator of all things worldly or material. Dualism often emphasized battles of opposites: good versus evil; light versus darkness. Other Gnostics believed that their goal was to transition out of the body created by the "evil God" and become "one with the good God." Consequently some supported the concept of reincarnation, believing that the soul could endure multiple iterations in the impure physical condition. Gnostics in general felt that many religions had the capacity to reveal truth.

As you might expect, Gnosticism was vehemently denied and refuted by New Testament authors and by early Church leaders. But it was indeed the basis for numerous other variations subsequently labeled as heresies. Valentinian Gnosticism was one such variation.

Valentinus (ca. 100–ca.153), a disgruntled would-be bishop according to Tertullian, abandoned the established Church and founded his own faith. This brilliant and eloquent man was successful in starting schools in Egypt, Cyprus, and Rome. Highlights of his teachings included a belief that Sophia made a mistake in creating the Universe, that we need to escape from bodily prison and return to the Eternal Being, that Christ as redeemer guides us back to that Being through gnosis, that Jesus was pure spirit, that redemption is preordained, and that only humanity's upper echelon could be redeemed. This is an oversimplified summary of a complex neo-platonic system of beliefs, but suffice to say the Church recognized the dangers of Valentinianism. According to Elaine Pagels in *The Gnostic Gospels*, those who followed Valentinus "shared a religious vision of the nature of God that they found incompatible with the rule of priests and bishops that was emerging in the Catholic Church—and so they resisted it." And that, dear readers, hit a nerve in the Church hierarchy.

It is not clear where or with any precision when Valentinus died, but he was proclaimed a heretic around 175, after his death.

Origen of Alexandria (ca. 185–254) is described by Pagels (*Gnostic Gospels*, p. 147) as the most brilliant theologian of the third century. He was not condemned as a heretic, but some of his theological views were condemned by Church Councils and his philosophy eventually just disappeared. He took the Christian theory of redemption and created a philosophical system (Johnson, p. 111), applying a positive spin. Hailing Christianity as a message for all humans, he depicted God as one who encouraged all people to improve themselves and to aim for perfection. He rejected the theory that God offers salvation to only the social and intellectually elite. The post-Constantine Church rejected Origen's optimism, however, opting for a gloomier view of the chances for redemption.

It is significant to mention Manichaeism as well, because Augustine was a believer in it for a time—until his formal rejection of this Gnostic movement in 384. An early influence during the beginning days of Christianity and surviving into the Middle Ages, this religion was created by a Persian named Mani (ca. 216–276). A peculiar mix of Persian Magi teachings, Gnosticism, and Christianity, Manichaeism was marked by the following characteristics:

1. Dualism (Kingdoms of Light and Darkness)

2. Belief that all religions are equally valid

3. Belief (Docetism) that Christ was divine but appeared to be human.

4. Promoting the concept of reincarnation and life cycles

5. Teaching the necessity for strict asceticism

Manichaeism also exhibited extreme pessimism regarding the potential of human nature and inherent goodness, with the exception of a godly elite (Johnson, p. 114). This secretive heresy should sound familiar since it was reflected in Augustine's teachings that we have already addressed. Some of the Manichean concepts persisted in the form of other heresies.

Heresy became punishable by death in 382, well after the Nicene Council of 325 and the establishment of the church-state. Ordered by the Emperor Magnus Maximus, the first victim of execution for heresy was believed to be Priscillian, Bishop of Avila, a Spanish ascetic said to practice astrology and preach dualism. Ambrose of Milan and Martin of Tours protested his execution, not for the act itself but for the process. They felt the Church had the right to punish its own. Ironically, the Church later made a habit of handing over heretics to the state for punishment to avoid bloodying its own hands.

The Beguines

During the Middle Ages when knights headed off to Crusades for glory and salvation, women's choices were limited to wifely responsibilities or cloistered convents. Both required subservience to men. Although the date is uncertain, sometime between 1150 and 1170 groups of women spontaneously came together in northern Europe to achieve an objective in between these options. Not accepted as full participants in the movements of Dominic (ca. 1170–1221) and Francis of Assisi (ca. 1181–1226), the phenomenon of the Beguines, with no specific organization or founder, served their spiritual goals and altruistic needs.

These women came from diverse backgrounds, some married, some widowed, some single, as well as some with children. The flexibility of the movement also accommodated the choice to remain in or leave the Beguinages to marry. A limited number of men called Beghards were also attracted to the movement, which allowed them to pursue a committed life without taking formal vows. Celibacy was also by choice.

The Beguines never became an "approved" religious order, although they did receive some special privileges and exemptions usually awarded such orders. The lack of formal vows is what ultimately brought their undoing. Church hierarchy took issue with the amount of apparent freedom and flexibility the women enjoyed. The Church's suspicion of the Beguine movement led to its condemnation as heretical, despite the fact that most Beguines considered themselves orthodox. During their time of existence, they were devoted to the Eucharist, sought simplicity, and pursued charitable works to the admiration of many.

In an essay on the Beguines, Elizabeth T. Knuth expresses her intrigue with the movement (http://www.users.csbsju.edu/~eknuth/xpxx/beguines. html). She notes that they arrived on the scene at a time of "religious ferment," along with protest movements, the Waldensians, Lollards, Brothers and Sisters of the Free Spirit, Spiritual Franciscans, Apostolici, Albigensians, Joachimites, and Flagellants.

Knuth goes on to say that the Beguines met their demise in several steps. First: The Fourth Lateran Council of 1216 ruled against the founding of any new religious orders. Second: The Second Council of Lyons in 1274 cited the Beguines for violation of this ruling. Third: The Council of Vienne (1311–12) specifically called the Beguines heretical, associating them with the Free Spirit heresy whose goal was to avoid sin in early life and reach union with God. The same document claimed, however, that it was perfectly acceptable for women penitents to form communities without taking vows. Finally, in 1318 the Bishop of Cologne mandated dissolution of all Beguine groups, requiring their association with approved Orders. The Beguines' property was subsequently confiscated and unmarried women were required to marry! Although some Beguinages still existed in Belgium and Holland in 1969, the Church succeeded in squelching a movement that promoted spiritual and intellectual development of women unsupervised, for all intents and purposes, by men. Do you suppose they were viewed as a threat?!

Heresy and the Albigensian Crusade (1209–1229)

Until 1204, Crusades had been called against the actions and faith of Islamic infidels in the Holy Land. The Albigensian Crusade, however, was an internal crusade to "protect the faith" against the Albigensian heresy in the southern part of France.

Called Albigensian for the city of Albi, believers were also called Cathars. Inhabitants of this wealthy and cultured movement were attracted to the Cathar movement similar to Manichaeism, which emphasized duality of good and evil. The heresy lay in the belief that Jesus had not lived in bodily form. Some research also indicates that Cathars revered Mary Magdalene and believed she was the partner of Jesus. That belief, of course, could not be tolerated. It was against the Cathars, a.k.a. Albigensians, that the Church launched both a Crusade and an Inquisition. Parenthetically, there are some who confuse the Cathars with the Templars, but as Karen Ralls reminds us in the *Knights Templar Encyclopedia*, the Templars were a military religious order whose views were more orthodox than those of the Cathars. The Templars also met an unsavory fate at the hands of the Pope, as we will discuss later.

The Albigensian/Cathar heresy was so pervasive in the Languedoc region of France that a nervous Pope Innocent III called for a crusade to squelch the escalating movement, after the unsuccessful efforts of droves of priests sent to convert the heretics. The Cathars had formerly enjoyed the support of local nobles and of bishops resenting papal authority. But the nobles were excommunicated and the bishops suspended, replaced by papal legates—all actions laying the groundwork for an attack. The Pope easily recruited volunteers, including many unsavory characters from northern France. They were no doubt enticed by the many "perks," such as gifts of confiscated lands and wealth, plenary indulgences, and a moratorium on debts for any existing agreements.

As the "crusade" progressed, leaders in 1209 actually bragged about showing no mercy to "order, age, or sex" in killing more than fifteen thousand in the "miraculous capture of Beziers." One of the crusaders reputedly asked his leader how to identify the heretics. The response was, "Kill them all. God will know his own!" The horrific quote has been attributed by some to Simon de Montfort, Captain General of French Forces in the Crusades against the Albigenses but more likely was uttered by Arnaud Amoury (Arnaud Amalric) Cistercian Abbot-Commander and Papal Legate to Pope Innocent III (http://www.languedoc-france.info/120502_arnaud.htm; http://www.time. com/time/magazine/article/0,9171,897752-2,00.html). There are discrepancies in reports of who actually said those words, especially since the Church would like to disavow them; but the events were recorded by "sympathetic fellow churchmen" as well as by those sympathetic to the crusaders in *The Song of the Cathar Wars*. According to that piece, French crusaders fully intended to launch a "popular terrorist tactic of indiscriminate massacre"

(http://www.catharcastles.info/120701_beziers.htm). Far too many passionate Crusaders were accustomed to brutality and slaughter in the name
of their religion. Johnson (p. 252) says that prisoners were mutilated, blinded,
dragged by horses, and used as target practice. The outrage of the brutality
probably added to the length of the conflict as the besieged Cathars battled to
survive. The twenty-year-long onslaught ended in the crushing destruction
of Albigensian culture and ultimately led to the creation of the Inquisition.

There were those still in Church favor who protested the brutality of the
"crusade" and the lack of recourse given to Cathari who were burned on the
spot. Matrons refusing to succumb to the lusts of priests were added to the
Cathar death list; wealthy Cathari were released after relinquishing substan-
tial funds; others were burned for refusing to endure the ordeal of a hot iron.
The treatment of heretics was inconsistent, however, and from 1180–1230
the Church created a codified system for dealing with suspected heretics. The
concept was conceived as an attempt at reform but in reality incorporated
many of the old practices and added new ones.

While the first wave of sorting out heresies occurred during the formation of the official Church Canon, the second wave was greatly in response
to reformers objecting to the power and (some felt) obscene affluence of the
Church. The yearning to return to the simpler days of Christianity served as
a catalyst for dissent. Disobedience was not an option when dealing with the
Church, which also acted as a political whip.

Inquisition: the Components

Just mentioning the word "Inquisition" evokes a visceral reaction and images
of twisted suspicion, tortured confessions, and burnings at the stake. Inquisition literally means a questioning or examination, but the one with claim on
the name actually was a court instituted by the medieval Church to root out
and deal with heretics. The medieval Church defended its creation based on
past biblical practices and the theories of Augustine, who interpreted Luke
14:23 as sanction. Aquinas supports extermination of heretics in *Summa
Theologica:*

> ... Wherefore if forgers of money and other evil-doers are forthwith
> condemned to death by secular authority, much more reason is there

for heretics, as soon as they are convicted of heresy, to be not only excommunicated but even put to death.

Simply put, Karen Ralls in her *Knights Templar Encyclopedia* describes heresy during the Middle Ages as "a religious belief or opinion in opposition to the orthodox doctrine of the Church." She goes on to say that Inquisition Prosecutors were less interested in determining the truth about accused heretics than they were in finding them guilty as accused by the Church. Biased witnesses and torturous treatments were used to accomplish that goal.

The Inquisition essentially consisted of four distinct yet interconnected elements:

1. The "Medieval Inquisition" is viewed in two sections, the Episcopal Inquisition (1184 – ca. 1230) and the Papal Inquisition (ca. 1230– late fourteenth century) that was created to address the shortcomings of the Episcopal Inquisition.

2. The "Spanish Inquisition" (1478–1834) is often considered the most brutal. It was begun and in its most violent stages controlled by Spanish monarchs King Ferdinand and Queen Isabella of Castile, with approval from Pope Sixtus IV. This Inquisition differed from other Inquisitions in that it was under royal control and staffed by secular clergy.

3. Pope Paul III established the "Roman Inquisition" in 1542 for the purpose of maintaining and defending the integrity of the faith and to review and determine courses of action to address errors and false doctrines.

4. The "Portuguese Inquisition," an offshoot of the Spanish Inquisition, was established in 1536 by Portuguese King Joao.

The first medieval inquisition was established around 1184 by a papal bull called "Ad abolendam," which translates as "For the purpose of doing away with," and was aimed at suppressing heresies in southern France and northern Italy. This inquisition was referred to as an *episcopal inquisition*, conducted by regional bishops. It proved ineffective, because bishops came infrequently and from long distances and were often preoccupied with other duties. Furthermore, the papal bull required that the name of the accuser be revealed, often creating local actions of revenge even before the trials were started.

In their early form, inquisitions were often instigated by secular rulers with less than admirable motivations, often including desires for power and wealth. The onslaught brought against the Cathari was actually prompted by King Philip II of France, who was envious of the riches in southern France and calculated a devious plan to usurp them. Despite brutal atrocities conducted against the Cathars, their heresy persisted, inciting Pope Gregory IX to call in the experts. Papal Inquisitors, mostly Dominicans and Franciscans, newly formed orders of friars, were sent to the afflicted area and given carte blanche authority to handle the situation. By 1231, *the* Inquisition was formally underway with a handbook of rules designed to provide consistency to the process. This phase was known as the *Papal Inquisition.*

Much of what we know about how the Inquisition operated can be seen in the *Handbook for Inquisitors* developed by Bernard Gui in the beginning of the fourteenth century. Gui was a Dominican friar and an Inquisitor who lived in Toulouse during the reign of Pope Gregory IX (1227–1241). He developed a technique that was used as a model for extracting confessions from the accused. In describing characteristics of an Inquisitor, he charges that, "He ought to be diligent and fervent in his zeal for religious truth, the salvation of souls and the extirpation of heresy." An Inquisitor should also be calm, courageous, and circumspect during the process. He concludes the paragraph saying, "Let the love of truth and mercy, which ought always to dwell in the heart of the judge, shine on his countenance, so that his decisions may never be dictated by envy or by cruelty." From what history tells us, theory and practice did not always mesh.

The *Spanish Inquisition* targeted converted Muslims, Jews, and illuminists and also led to the Peruvian Inquisition and the Mexican Inquisition. We will discuss their motives, methods, and atrocities later.

Inquisition: the Process

In the thirteenth century, Inquisitors would arrive in an area suspected of housing heretical beliefs. As part of their investigation, they would gather all the citizens of the town into a public place. Whether or not they were heretics, townspeople must have been terrified to see the Inquisitors arrive.

Attendance was referred to as voluntary, but absence might cause suspicion! All were urged to "rat" on their neighbors.

There was typically a month-long grace period, during which penitent heretics could confess and avoid persecution by revealing fellow heretics. After the grace period, denunciations were reviewed and the accused were summoned to appear before the Inquisitors and witnesses (whose names had been concealed). Suspects were then examined.

Only two witnesses were required to make an accusation, and their names were withheld from the accused to avoid future reprisal. The accused was allowed to construct a list of his enemies who were supposed to be discounted by the Inquisitors. The defendant was also allowed to have a lawyer at the trial, but a conviction meant that the lawyer would lose his license to practice law. Few were eager to take the risk.

A papal bull in 1252 from Innocent IV approved the use of torture to achieve confessions, although bloodshed, mutilation, and death were forbidden. Use of such horrific torture was commonplace in the medieval judicial system, however. But an article entitled "Understanding the Inquisition," published online in *Catholic World News,* claims that the role of the Inquisitor was not to extract confessions from "unwilling witnesses" but to persuade heretics to "recognize their errors and return to the Catholic faith."

Though the bull approving torture included restrictions, there is documentation that physical torture conducted by Inquisitors was often used to coerce the accused into confessing. Such procedures as stretching limbs on a rack, burning with live coals, squeezing of fingers and toes, and the strappado vertical rack could achieve amazing results. Use of the strappado involved tying hands behind the back with ropes and suspending the accused in such a way as to dislocate the joints in both arms. Weights could also be added to dislocate the legs! As horrific as those tortures sound, they reputedly were not as bad as those inflicted by governments.

Robert Lerner, author of *The Heresy of the Free Spirit in the Later Middle Ages,* references brutal tactics used to elicit confessions as indicated in Inquisitorial records. He asserts that torture absolutely influenced and distorted testimony; he further contends that even those who were not tortured were influenced by the imminent threat of "the stake." Lerner says that confession guaranteed mercy from capital punishment (pp. 4–5) and conversions were considered prizes to Inquisitors. The more elaborate the confession, the more likely the judges would be to "grant absolution and a mild penance." He also insinuates an intriguing theory regarding "confessing personalities." Interrogations invoke a reaction in some individuals that induces them to confess to crimes they did not commit.

In the process of determining guilt of potential heretics, then, there could be false witnesses with axes to grind, excruciating torture designed to force confessions, and innocent defendants who were susceptible to confessing.

Standardized questions were used, according to surviving Inquisitors' manuals; checklists and official minutes of inquisitions have also been preserved. Lerner claims that the procedures produced stereotyped testimony from the prescribed set of questions deemed appropriate for the suspected heresy. Each heresy had its own set of questions, with no accommodation for the "square peg," the anomaly that did not fit.

Suspects and witnesses were required to take an oath to tell all at the onset of the interrogation. Any hesitation would imply guilt. A person who confessed and submitted to the Inquisitors might escape with minor penalties such as flogging, fasts, pilgrimages, or fines. More serious punishments are described below.

Lerner also weighs in (p. 5) on the protocol for recording the responses to the questions. According to him, notes were not made verbatim, but indicated highlights of the interview—that is, points considered most significant by the scribe or Inquisitor. Furthermore, despite the fact that most interviews were conducted in the vernacular, they were recorded in Latin, allowing for errors and miscommunication. Joan of Arc was supposedly interrogated by two men behind a curtain who recorded everything incriminating her and left out information excusing her. Furthermore, the scribe was required to change the meaning of French words when translating them into Latin (Lerner, p. 5), obviously skewing the actual interrogation.

Consequences and Punishment

After the conclusion of the trial, defendants were detained in prisons until the results were revealed. That process could conceivably take years, as the Inquisitors would wait until they had enough cases to announce in a public ceremony called "sermo generalis" or "general address." They handed down a variety of punishments including long pilgrimages, wearing the yellow cross for a lifetime, confiscation of property, banishment, imprisonment, and public recantation.

The Synod of Verona in 1184 proclaimed that burning was the official punishment for heresy, a decision that was upheld by subsequent Councils and Synods throughout the 1600s. Burning at the stake was reserved for the most serious offenders, however: those who refused to repent and those who had "relapsed." Wearing the yellow cloth cross, the "cross of infamy" and symbol of a former heretic, was a stigma of social ostracism and offenders could not find employment. The punishment of the yellow cross was a form of "enforced recantation." Failing to wear it meant failure to acknowledge guilt and therefore was perceived as a relapse into heresy and a violation of the judgment. The poor souls were in a no-win situation. Later Puritan women were branded with a scarlet A for their adulterous sins and were shunned by townspeople, but wearers of the yellow cross were ostracized because any individuals associating with them could also be accused as heretics.

Since the Church was forbidden to shed blood, the condemned heretics were transferred to secular authorities for execution, usually burning at the stake. Executioners readily obliged their Christian duty and recognized that burning did not violate the law prohibiting bloodshed. The burnings (or hangings) were conducted in Romanesque spectacle, witnessed by all the area townspeople.

There is some dispute regarding the number of heretics who were actually burned at the stake, since the Inquisition's responsibilities were extended to include sorcery, alchemy, blasphemy, sexual aberration, and infanticide. It appears that after the late fifteenth century there were many more witches and sorcerers burned at the stake than heretics. Witchcraft became equated with heresy when Church coffers began to decline.

Familiar Heretics

Many heretics suffered the consequences of the Inquisition's zeal, including familiar historical figures Giordano Bruno, Galileo, Joan of Arc, and the Knights Templar.

We all know about Joan of Arc, the Maid of Orleans, who rallied an army to put the rightful king on the throne of France. She listened to saintly voices giving her instructions for victory in battle. Overconfidence got the best of her, however, and she drove her troops far beyond capacity and need. She let ego, rather than divine guidance, be her guide.

Her enemies focused attention on her shortcomings and reported her to the Inquisitors. She was after all a woman wearing men's clothing. It was surely appropriate to wear pants and armor when leading troops into battle, but women were not allowed to "wear the pants" in those days except briefly for travel. She also offended the Inquisitors by dealing directly with God and the saints. (Remember, lay people were supposed to use priests as intermediaries!)

Fifty-seven interrogators, including some Englishmen Joan had offended earlier, employed a method designed to convict her. Originally charged with seventy counts including sorcery and witchcraft, the charge was reduced to twelve counts which the Inquisitors supposedly "proved." Giving in to a relentless grilling and fearing death, she recanted her earlier protestations and admitted guilt. Joan confessed to previous sins of "falsely pretending to have had revelations from God and his angels, St. Catherine and St. Margaret." She contritely sought mercy and renewed union with the Church. Her "confession" of guilt saved her, at least temporarily, from the fire as she was sentenced to life imprisonment. But the English guards removed her female clothing leaving her with only male attire. The ecclesiastical court interpreted her masculine dress as relapse into heresy and condemned her to death. In 1431 Joan was burned at the stake, still waiting for her loyal rescuers to arrive. The Church eventually rescinded the verdict in 1455 and proclaimed her a saint in 1920.

Both Giordano Bruno (1548–1600) and Galileo (1564–1642) were suspect because of their subscription to the ideas of Copernicus.

Bruno, an Italian philosopher, astronomer/astrologer, spy, and occultist, was also charged with Docetism, a belief that Jesus did not have a physical body. Revered by the science world as a martyr for his rejection of geocentrism, Bruno refused to recant his beliefs and was executed accordingly: gagged, hung upside down, and burned.

Galileo also rejected geocentrism, the approved Church theory that earth was the center of the universe. His use of a new Dutch invention called a telescope gave him insights about the universe and prompted his support of Copernicus' heliocentric theory that earth and the other planets revolve around the sun. The Roman Inquisition targeted Galileo in 1633, based on Pope Urban III's contention that Galileo was connected to Bruno. Galileo was convicted by the Inquisition and required to recant his support of Copernican theory. Galileo did make a full confession and was sentenced to life imprisonment, mostly because of his elderly status. He lived out the remainder of his life under house arrest at his home in Florence.

In 1992, three hundred fifty years after Galileo's death, Pope John Paul II acknowledged errors made by the theological advisors during the trial of Galileo; but he failed to admit any wrongdoing on the Church's part for convicting Galileo on a heretical charge of promoting heliocentrism. The Galileo case was declared closed.

The Knights Templar have become familiar to many because of numerous books written about them in the last decade. Their controversy and mystery continue to intrigue us. Founded as an international military order during the Crusades, the Knights evolved as protectors for pilgrims on the way to the Holy Land; they also became the first "bankers" entrusted with the money and treasures of others.

On Friday, October 13, 1307, agents of King Philip IV of France rounded up and arrested for heretical behavior nearly all Knights Templar in France. "Philip the Fair" as he was called, threatened by the power and presence of the Knights in his country and tempted by their presumed wealth, convinced Pope Clement V to permit the arrests and confiscation of funds. He allegedly succeeded in catching the Templars completely by surprise by sealing the orders for his soldiers until just before the actions were to be carried out.

Lynn Picknett and Clive Prince, authors of *The Templar Revelation*, comment on the apparently "bloodless coup d'état" against some of Christendom's best-trained warriors (p. 109) and question why the Templars didn't call in reinforcements from outside France. They also indicate that some of the Knights did escape, including the Order's treasurer, an indication that there had been a "tip-off." They also cite the mysterious "disappearance" of the renowned Templar fleet which had been based in France until then. Where did they go? Mystery still clouds the truth but speculation abounds!

Of those who were rounded up, many Knights confessed to a myriad of bizarre behaviors and beliefs allegedly justifying their arrest. But once again the element of torture surely influenced their confessions, as the hot irons got closer to their faces and limbs. In 1310, fifty-four Templars were burned at the stake. Despite the fact that Clement was not certain that there was enough evidence to prove heresy, he continued to allow the persecution to continue. Ultimately the Pope gave in to the King and dissolved the "Poor Knights of the Temple" in 1312 and executed Jacques de Molay, the Knights' last Grand Master.

There are indications that the Church considered the Templar persecution unjust, that the Templars had done nothing wrong, and that the Pope was manipulated into suppressing them. In 2002, Dr. Barbara Frale reputedly found what is called the Chinon Parchment in the Secret Vatican Archives. The document indicates that Pope Clement V secretly pardoned the Knights Templar in 1314.

The Spanish Inquisition

Torquemada. The name itself sends chills down the spine and is often equated with the most cruel and fanatic aspects of the Inquisition. Tomas de Torquemada was Queen Isabella's confessor and First Grand Inquisitor of Spain. The Dominican monk is "credited" with the expulsion of Jews in 1492 and was responsible for the burning of 8800 people and the punishment/torture of 9654 others. The *Catholic Encyclopedia* disputes these numbers and cites claims of other historians who state that from 1485–1498, "more than 2000 Jews were burned as impenitent sinners." This contrary view of course purports that other claims were inflated and exaggerated. Torquemada's charge was the preservation of "Christian Spain," although he is said to have had Jewish heritage in his genealogy. His rigidly hard rules and strict adherence to them earned Torquemada his reputation for cruelty.

The Spanish Inquisition was not only ruthless; it was also relentless and survived for many years, essentially because it was self-sufficient thanks to the confiscated properties of the convicted heretics. The need for money to continue its existence fed the need for more convictions and thus "justified" the use of increased torture to achieve those convictions. When suspects began to wane, the Inquisition raised funds from informers or "familiars" who paid a fee for immunity from arrest along with other privileges.

Spain's intolerance and hatred had been directed first at Moors and Jews, and then broadened to include Protestants, foreigners, and those of "impure blood." Hatred and fear of Jews began to subside in northern regions, however, as a new target was established: Many presumed heretics had escaped to the mountains and the heresy hunt was extended to a "witch-hunt" in remote regions. Witches had been dismissed as pagan superstition during the Dark Ages, and Charlemagne had made witch-hunting unlawful. During the thirteenth century, however, the Dominican Inquisition revisited that posture and created a new category of heretics, presumably to increase funds when old ones ran out.

Although the Spanish Inquisition was abolished in 1834, its shocking impacts remain in our collective awareness.

According to "Understanding the Inquisition," the Vatican opened the Inquisition archives in 1998 to scholars in an attempt to provide a "more balanced understanding." Originally called "the Sacred Congregation of the Roman and Universal Inquisition" in 1542, the name was changed in 1908 to the Holy Office by Pope Pius X. Pope Paul VI in 1967 changed the duties of the office and changed its name to the Congregation for the Doctrine of the Faith.

Evolution of Witch-hunts

Witch. What image comes to mind when you see or hear that word? Is it a big-nosed hag with a wart, wearing black robes, pointed hat, and riding a broom across the night sky? Was the image that came to mind influenced by *The Wizard of Oz or Wicked*? To be sure, creative authors, playwrights, and movie producers have helped shape our image of what a witch looks like.

Regardless of the image, the word "witch" has come to us with a generally negative connotation and scary image. The etymology is far less intimidating. What was done to "witches," and those suspected of being witches, during the Middle Ages in Europe and in the early days of the American colonies is *truly* frightening. False accusations led to unspeakable tortures for innocent victims.

Matilda Gage (p. 236) says that the word "witch" used to mean "a woman of superior knowledge" according to vast information available at that time. She later substantiates that definition, citing Henry More, a seventeenth-century Cambridge scholar who defined a witch as a "wise or learned woman" according to etymological research. Witch is also derived from "wekken," to prophesy, justifying the meaning as seer.

Witches were most commonly associated with their ability to use herbs and herbal remedies for healing and alleviating pain. Their skill at reducing the mother's pain in childbirth ran counter to Church teachings that women suffer in childbirth because of their association with Eve's sin. According to Gage, using such remedies to mitigate the pains of childbirth was "proof of collusion with the devil" to Inquisitors (p. 242).

Gage also vehemently contends that since knowledge is often equated with power, the Church feared women's use of knowledge and therefore felt justified in its attack on women of intellect. She further states that death by torture was a method the Church employed for repressing women's intellect, since knowledge was considered evil and dangerous in her hands. One needs only to browse parts of *The Witch Hammer,* first published in 1486 by German zealot Inquisitors Heinrich Kramer and Jacob (John) Sprenger, to sense the venom intended for all non-conformists, especially female ones. They even claimed that "femina" meant "one wanting in faith." Their interpretation of "femina" speaks for itself and underscores the bias.

It was in 1484 that Pope Innocent VIII appointed Kramer and Sprenger to be Inquisitors in northern Germany. The two were supposedly experts in witch-hunting, which quickly became their specialty. Together they assembled huge volumes of documented convictions of witches achieved with the use of torture. Based on their dossier, this "Traveling Witch Inquisition," as Gage calls them, effectively convinced Pope Innocent VIII to expand their power. By 1486 they published their alleged findings in *Malleus Maleficarum,* translated "Witch Hammer," which became a fifteenth-century bestseller.

Two events, namely acknowledgement by the Pope in 1484 that witchcraft was a *"crimen exceptum"* (i.e., "excepted crime") approving torture for the accused subjects and the publication of *The Witch Hammer,* contributed dramatically to the development of the European witch craze. The Pope designated practicing witchcraft a "crimen exceptum" because it was considered a dire threat against the safety and well-being of the people and required that

normal procedures be suspended. Furthermore, allegations made and confessions elicited under the duress of torture were represented as irrefutable
fact. (The approach sounds strangely current and reminiscent of the Bush
administration's handling of prisoners perceived to be potential terrorists!)
The Witch Hammer became a witch primer and the basis for misogynistic
misinformation and caricature representations of witches still felt in today's
Christian psyche and culture.

It is an outrageous fact that even prior to the actual "hunt," women
who were acknowledged witches—namely, wise women, midwives, and healers—were unfairly maligned and associated with the devil. So when the
Inquisition did begin, tens of thousands of women (and some men) were
swept easily into the net. They were hunted in the manner in which one
hunts wild animals to kill as sport, displaying the kill as trophies burning on
the stake or hanging from trees. The witch-hunts illustrate vividly the insane
and inhumane behavior employed in so many contexts for so-called religious
and misogynistic purposes.

It was easy to be considered a witch suspect. A man angry with his wife
could claim she was a witch; someone supporting a "so-called witch" was
also suspect. An old woman was a likely target. Women often lived longer
than men, becoming a perceived burden on society while contributing little
in the minds of the community. Men were especially curious about a witch's
appearance. They reasoned that it must be someone who looked different
from other people, for example women with eyes of a different color than
what was most common. In Spain and Italy a blue-eyed woman was suspect.
Women with red hair were definitely witch material. Red-haired women often
had freckles that could be construed as "witch marks." The "witch's mark"
was supposed to be the clincher and a sign that the victim had indulged in an
amorous relationship with the devil. Inquisitors would examine the victim's
body for such a mark after stripping her. The executioner would shave all her
body hair in order to reveal the mark in her formerly "hidden parts." Warts,
freckles, and birthmarks were identified as signs of her guilt but the absence
of a mark was no guarantee of innocence.

A person accused of being a witch was in a lose/lose situation. She
would be tortured twice, three times, four times until she finally confessed.
Recantation of the confession was determined to be perjury. Robert Lerner's

"confessor's personality" theory is borne out in documented stories referenced by Barbara Walker in *The Woman's Encyclopedia of Myths and Secrets* (p. 1004).

Walker describes a woman who, despite her innocence, confessed to the Inquisitors that she was a witch. She later told her private confessor that she never dreamed she could possibly admit to something she hadn't done; she was not a witch; she had not seen the devil. She had even incriminated others who were innocent when threatened with further pain.

Torture was used "extensively, viciously, and persistently breaking all but the most heroic spirits." A physician serving in witch prisons recounted firsthand accounts of women driven mad "by frequent torture, prolonged squalor and darkness of dungeons, amid recurring torture." Even motherhood was a liability, according to Walker, since children were susceptible to the threat of torture and could be easily manipulated into incriminating their mothers.

Johnson (p. 309) says that witches replaced Jews as objects of hate and fear, and that torture was the key ingredient for the success and continuation of witch-hunts. According to him, there was a direct correlation between the amount of torture and the number of convictions: As torture was relaxed, convictions decreased.

Johnson also argues that there was a relationship between the escalation of witch-hunts and Catholic-Reformer strife. The latter half of the fifteenth century marked an explosion of witch-hunts, as each side accused the other of heresy. Most German reformers had accepted the witchcraft myth as fact; Luther himself felt that burning witches was an appropriate action for their dealings with the devil, and actually had four burned at Wittenburg. The Calvinists, however, took the prize for witch-hunts. According to Johnson (p. 310), witches were systematically hunted down where Calvinism took hold. Also in contention for the prize were the followers of Ignatius Loyola, a puritanical Catholic who was also a zealous witch-hunter. The ultimate "winner" of witch-hunts goes to Johann Georg II Fuchs von Dornheim, who burned six hundred witches in Bamburg, Germany, in 1628.

The Peace of Westphalia in 1648 ended thirty years of major fighting in Europe and promoted a more reasoned approach, one result being that witch-hunting soon was no longer an international craze. Furthermore, scientific theories about natural phenomena began to undo the underpinnings of witch-hunts. Nonetheless, pockets of witch-hunting flared where hot spots and festering circumstances managed to prevail. Johnson (p. 312), for example, cites the defection of Queen Christina to Rome as an inflammatory act in Sweden in the 1660s prompting witch-hunts. Protestant Switzerland conducted the last "legal" witch burning in 1782 followed by an illegal one in Catholic Poland a decade later.

Witch-hunts in the New World

As we are well aware, witch-hunts did not end at European borders. Some of the very same unjust aspects of European Christianity were incorporated into the tenets of the early American colonies. Puritans fleeing persecution in their native lands brought with them the same "spirit of persecution" supporting the theory that all women are inferior and inherently wicked as taught by the Church they fled (Gage, p. 282). They brought with them a belief in witchcraft as well.

Blending religious and judicial punishment, the Massachusetts Colony initiated laws against those suspected of witchcraft. (Witchcraft was usually equated with women, although some men were also accused.) Women were ordered to be stripped naked and examined by a "witch pricker" who searched for the devil's mark. These escaped Puritans also persecuted old women and coerced young children to act as witnesses against their mothers accused of witchcraft or imprisoned the children on suspicion as well.

We all learned about the Salem Witch Trials in school and are aware of the lies and convolutions that led to the hanging or burning of innocent people in Salem, Massachusetts, in 1692. Ironically "Salem" (a variation of "shalom") came from a Semitic word meaning peace. (Jerusalem actually means "House of Peace"!) Gage (p. 283) claims that Boston, which she calls "The Bloody Town," rivaled Salem in its persecution of women who expressed thoughts contrary to Puritanical beliefs. Such independent thinkers were publicly whipped at whipping posts. New England was already cemented in its conformity of religious opinion (Gage, p. 283), a position that led to the Vagabond Law of the Massachusetts Colony in 1661, punishing "free thought."

Imagine that. The very people who left Europe for religious freedom would inflict punishment on other people who also sought religious freedom.

Anne Hutchinson led the first real struggle for a woman's religious liberty. In a witch-hunt of a different type, twenty-four charges were brought against her, including her audacity to "teach men." (As noted earlier, women were forbidden to preach or teach religious information, according to 1 Timothy 2:11 and 1 Corinthians 14:34–35. 1 Timothy 2:12–14 says, "I do not permit a woman to teach or to have authority over a man. She must be quiet. For Adam was formed first; then Eve. Further, Adam was not deceived, but woman was deceived and transgressed" (NAB). This charge apparently came about because of instructional sessions held in her own home in which sixty to a hundred women listened to Anne's critiques of both Sunday sermons and Thursday lectures (Gage, p. 286). The sessions were reportedly so interesting that men began to attend.

Gage says that the First Ecclesiastical Convocation met in America to specifically consider the religious views of Mrs. Hutchinson. As a result, in November of 1637 the Massachusetts General Court accused Hutchinson of sedition and heresy. She was questioned, imprisoned, and finally banished from the colony. Many other women were subsequently silenced, persecuted for the "crime" of free speech!

Hutchinson, along with Roger Williams, a champion of religious freedom, sought safety in an area that later became Rhode Island, the state Williams founded, but a place the orthodox called "the sewer of New England" (Johnson, p. 423).

Gage called Boston "The Bloody Town" because in her opinion it was "the center of persecuting spirit and every species of wanton cruelty upon women." Massachusetts actually lost its charter in 1684 as a punishment for intolerance (Gage, p. 288). The Massachusetts Colony was not alone in its treatment of witchcraft, however. Eight of the original thirteen colonies actually recognized witchcraft as a capital crime: Virginia, Delaware, Maryland, South Carolina, Pennsylvania, New Jersey, Massachusetts, and New York. Gage cites numerous historical examples to illustrate witchcraft allegations against women in those states (p. 289).

Connecticut, my own home state, is not immune from the bigotry. The

September 27, 2007 edition of the *Hartford Courant* highlights a show called "The Witching Hour" about scapegoating in Hartford, Connecticut. Staff writer Matt Egan discussed the show's story based on Katherine Harrison, a woman accused of witchcraft. Ultimately banished from her home in Wethersfield, Connecticut, Katherine was a widowed landowner who was interested in astrology and fortune-telling. The seventeenth-century Puritans were not amused by her frankness and were envious of her wealth. As a result, she became the target of fear and intolerance. There surely were other examples of such banishing.

Witch-hunts in New England began to subside as new laws repealed those making witchcraft a crime. The English Parliament had repealed its statute against witchcraft in 1736. New England colonies gradually began to repeal witchcraft laws as well. Walker claims that the real reason that the idea of witchcraft persisted is that "Christian authorities couldn't let it die, without admitting that God's word was wrong and God's servants had committed millions of legal murders and tortured millions of helpless people without cause" (pp. 1087–88).

Some people have viewed the witch-hunts as gendercide. Based on the tens of thousands who died, approximately eighty percent of whom were women, a case could be made. Witch-hunts succeeded in making certain that women knew their places and stayed there. According to Walker, women of outstanding reputation in any field were at risk since female accomplishment was considered "symptomatic" of witchcraft. She underscores the Church's war on female healers: Healing was labeled a crime punishable by death if practiced by a woman, banning women from going to medical school. Those who healed without the proper training were branded as witches and condemned to die. Walker states that the history of witchcraft indicates that men persecuted women to retain their monopoly on profitable enterprises in the medical field and others (p. 1089).

Writing in the 1880s and 1890s, Gage is discouraged that "woman still suffers from the continuing superstition that she brought sin to the world." Accusing and condemning mostly women for witchcraft helped perpetuate the myth of woman's inherent evil and responsibility for Original Sin. And what can we say about that superstition today? Has it truly dissipated, or does that opinion remain latent in the rhetoric of today's politics and religion? Are dissenters viewed as exercising free speech or are they painted as heretical and unpatriotic? Have women really achieved equal rights? How far have women really come? These are definitely topics to pursue.

Sadly, war and violence and the "blame game" seem to be cyclical. There are always some who are hungry for power and wealth and willing to "protect" some of us from a threatening Other; and there are always people willing to believe them. Blaming others, holding them accountable for misfortune or the unknown, is usually based on fear: Blame Eve. Blame woman. Blame heretics. Blame witches. Blame people who are different from you.

Contemplating the topics of this chapter, we know that philosophers and poets have long lamented "man's inhumanity to man." Intolerance and greed are surely at its root, but misogyny has undeniably influenced the ugly and reprehensible acts we have described here.

4

Christianity's Lost Leaders and New Faces of Eve

New scholarship is revealing that women played significant roles in the development of Christianity. This chapter examines, in particular, the roles of Mother Mary and Mary Magdalene as leaders of the fledgling Christian movement. Why was their leadership marginalized and diminished by the Church hierarchy? What is the rationale for their designation as "New Eves"?

Further: Mother Mary is presented as Virgin and "Theotokos," the God-bearer; according to some, she and her son Jesus represent a second Adam and Eve who saved humankind from the sins of the first humans. Mary Magdalene, until 1969, was portrayed as the penitent whore and to some the perpetuation of Eve as temptress and sinner. These two Marys were presented as juxtaposed archetypes, the virgin and whore, and as a result were deprived of their three-dimensional status as early Church leaders. How did Church dogma inform such portrayals as it developed and, more importantly, how have such portrayals impacted the psyche of Christian women?

The two Marys in Christianity. The Biggies!! The Blessed Virgin Mary and Mary Magdalene. Both have had a profound influence on my personal life. My own mother was very devoted to the Blessed Mother and that rubbed off on me. I chose Mary for my Confirmation name, prayed the rosary, and joined the Children of Mary Sodality. Devotion to Mother Mary underscored the message of her son Jesus, buoyed my faith, and provided hope when circumstances seemed dire. Her intercession was powerful and her miracles were legendary. I didn't question it. I basked in her love.

I didn't discover Mary Magdalene until my middle age, as I searched for the Grail and became a truth seeker. New research on Magdalene's life and role in early Christianity struck me like Zeus' lightning bolt, and I became obsessed with finding information about her. The more I discovered, the more I loved and admired her. In my mind's eye she has become my sister and friend.

Both of these remarkable women were REAL women who lived two thousand years ago. I was inspired to capture their essences and to research and report the tremendous contributions they made to the Christian movement as teachers and leaders, rather than as contrived symbols.

In the process of unveiling them, we will investigate how the personas of Mother Mary and Mary Magdalene have evolved over time. Once unthinkable, Mother Mary is now being honored—and in some cases revered—in some Protestant denominations! What's more, modern biblical scholars are helping to reshape the image of Mary Magdalene.

Why has the liturgy been so slow to reflect these changes? What are the potential impacts on Christians of viewing such outstanding females in a new light?

The New Eves

As you recall, Augustine was the first to associate the expulsion from Eden with carnal knowledge and sex. The emergence of lust and the desire for sex was the direct result, according to him, of the first couple's arrogance in disobeying God's law. Eating from the tree of knowledge, from this viewpoint, seems to express a double entendre. We should now better understand why the expression "to know someone, in the biblical sense" means that people have engaged in intercourse. Recall that Augustine also firmly established the concept of Original Sin, convinced that the sins of Eve (and by the way Adam) were also transferred to all other humans.

As mentioned in the previous chapter, the Celtic monk Pelagius argued that the transgression of Adam and Eve was a personal sin and not transferable to others. He felt that people possess free will and can choose to sin or not to sin. Unlike his contemporary Augustine, Pelagius felt that men and women are *not* born with the stain of sin. If his premise were supported, however, humankind wouldn't need redemption—according to the thinking of the day. The Augustinian explanation of course made for a good deal more job security for clerics whereas Pelagius' view undermined the perceived purpose of Christianity.

According to Augustinian thinking as Christian doctrine evolved further, virginity was a gift to women and the virgin birth of Jesus was a necessity. Since conception requires sexual activity, Mother Mary had to be free from that "stain" in order to carry and deliver the Christ Child without sin. As such she supposedly broke Eve's curse, providing new life for believers. Mother Mary became the Blessed Virgin Mary and a second Eve in the opinion of the Church.

According to the Bible, after the Fall, Adam named his wife "Eve" which meant "the mother of all the *living*" (Genesis 3:20, italics mine). Christ's mother in her turn became the mother of all the *faithful* in ritual and devotion. Some writers interestingly point out that Ave, often associated in praise of Mary (Ave Maria) in prayer and song, is actually the reverse of Eva–the Latin equivalent of Eve.

In *Mary through the Centuries*, Jaroslav Pelikan documents an early reference to the "new Eve" (p. 42). According to him, Irenaeus (ca. 130 – ca. 200 CE), Bishop of Lyons, drew the Eve/Mary parallel as well. Pelikan claims it is unclear whether the concept was Irenaeus' own or if he was merely underscoring beliefs commonly held even earlier. The parallels begin with Adam as the "earthy" first man and Christ as the Second Adam and "Lord from Heaven." Furthermore, the disobedient actions of Eve and the obedient behavior of Mother Mary were actions of free will rather than coercion.

Pelikan cites a work of Irenaeus discovered during the twentieth century entitled *Proof of the Apostolic Preaching*, which carries the parallels even further. Comparing aspects found in Genesis and the gospels, Irenaeus plays with such potential parallels as the Garden of Eden/Garden of Gethsemane and Tree of Knowledge/tree of the cross. He concludes, "And Eve [had necessarily to be restored] in Mary, that a virgin by becoming the advocate of a virgin, should undo and destroy virginal disobedience by virginal obedience" (Pelikan, p. 43). So the contrast is complete. According to Irenaeus, Mary, the mother of Christ and "second Eve," willingly obeys God's messengers and maintains her virginity, a behavior which counteracts the original Eve's disobedience in the garden and subsequent loss of her virginity. The actions of Mother Mary cancelled the actions of Sinner Eve.

Pope Hippolytus (ca. 170 – ca. 236 CE) extended the concept of "New Eve" from Mary (Magdalene, implied) to all the female disciples whose devotion to Christ symbolizes the reversal of Eve's sin. Hippolytus views those women as representing the "Bride of Christ," a title often ascribed to Mother Mary by other Church Fathers. Credited with being the first Church Father to call her "apostle to the apostles," Hippolytus puts a spotlight on Mary Magdalene as a model of faithfulness, contrasting her faithfulness to the sin of Eve in the Garden. As the first witness to the Resurrection, Magdalene was called by Jesus to be the apostle of the apostles (John 20:1–18). Ambrose (ca. 340–397 CE), Bishop of Milan, also associates Mary Magdalene with the new Eve as the woman who clings to Christ, the new Tree of Life. Her loyalty overturns the so-called unfaithfulness of Eve in the garden.

Toward the end of the sixth century, Pope Gregory I notably conflated Luke's sinful woman with Mary Magdalene. This image came down the centuries in a variety of forms envisioned by artists. One that strikes me in particular appears in a sixteenth-century painting by Matthias Grünewald known as the Isenheim Altarpiece. It can be seen online at the Genesis of Eden Diversity Encyclopedia Web site (http://www.dhushara.com/book/bbint/bb/consum2.pdf). The site's author describes the painting as "the dead [second] Adam hanging on his accursed tree before the twin aspects of Eve, the 'virgin of purity' in the mother and the 'penitent sinner' in Magdalene." Hence we observe the schizophrenic representation of Mary Magdalene both as first witness and early Church leader versus the redeemed harlot and role model for sinners. Views about Mary Magdalene changed over time to suit Church hierarchical/political needs and reflect changing theological doctrine.

The Deuteronomic curse in 21:22 was the origin of assigning the "Tree of Life" metaphor to the cross: "And if a man have committed a sin worthy of death . . . thou hang him in a tree" (KJ). Also on this Web site, the author of *Consummating Eden* Part 3 claims that "Noli me tangere" is Christ's rejection of "Eve"/Magdalene, his companion. In this interpretation the author refers to Magdalene as the new Eve who became the repentant sinner as the "physical and sexual complement of Christ's identity," and as one "who remains in the physical world to witness the risen Christ of the heavenly kingdoms." The negative sexual representation of Magdalene's character in such artwork served to perpetuate the false conflation of Marys.

Contemporary author Margaret Starbird lovingly and wistfully envisions the second coming of the new Adam and Eve in the persons of Jesus and Mary Magdalene, restored to their proper places together in a healed world. In Starbird's words, "Perhaps we can picture them—the New Adam and the New Eve—holding hands in the garden restored" (http://www.cosmic gaia2012.com/resources.html).

The "New Eve" is also depicted in a third metaphorical way by some Catholic Church leaders and theologians. "Holy Mother Church" is personified as the New Eve and "Mother of All" who will be reunited with Jesus as his spouse. Liturgical music often refers to Jesus and his "bride" the Church, a concept that often puzzles the laity. That "New Eve" depiction seems to displace both the feminine role in Christianity and Starbird's vision. Sadly, woman does not receive equal status even at the end of time according to this rendition.

Female Foundations of Christianity

Many women helped lay the groundwork for the emerging Church, but these two women in particular played pivotal roles in establishing the foundations of Christianity: Mary, as the mother who gave birth, and Mary Magdalene, as the companion who witnessed the Resurrection.

It is amazing that despite the fact that Christianity depends so much on the roles of these two women, the roles of women in the Church have been marginalized at best and eliminated at worst.

Mother Mary—our Blessed Mother, The Blessed Virgin Mary—was elevated to the title of "Theotokos," god bearer, by Cyril of Alexandria at the contentious Council of Ephesus in June of 431. Later, at the First Lateran Council in 649, Pope Martin I proclaimed the perpetual virginity of Mary as Church dogma. Her Assumption has been celebrated on August 15 since the seventh century, but it wasn't until 1950 that Pope Pius XII proclaimed

Mary's Assumption as an article of faith. The Assumption, also referred to as the "Dormition" (falling asleep), celebrates Mother Mary's departure from life and her "bodily assumption" into heaven.

Mother Mary's persona was raised in stature over time and came to be revered by many—much to the chagrin of Protestant reformers who felt that reverence toward her had become worship. Even her physical image became modified in artwork as she was portrayed in a less curvy and more "modest" manner. Controlling Mother Mary's image, the Church required that artists portray her garb as a white dress with a light blue veil, with golden rays extending from her hands rather than from her chest. (The color red was reserved for Mary Magdalene!) At times the Blessed Mother seemed dehumanized, a wax figure on a pedestal.

Marina Warner, author of *Alone of All Her Sex*, argues that the misogynistic representation of Mary as perpetual virgin demonizes conception and childbirth and so prevents Christian women from emulating her (p. 337). According to Warner, Mary does not represent the true archetype of the typical female nature; she is a player in the Catholic Church's unyielding representation of the structure of society, driven by a "God-given code." Warner also notes that in 1974 Pope Paul VI attempted to reinvent the image of Mother Mary into an updated model that would appeal to twentieth-century women. He referred to her as a multi-dimensional person, "champion of the oppressed and a woman of action and resolve" (p. 338). Pope Paul VI says that Mary is not simply consumed with her divine Son but rather she is "a woman whose action helped strengthen the apostolic community's faith in Christ." But Warner complains that the Church cannot simply reinvent the image of Mother Mary without owning up to its misrepresentations of the past, namely that women must bear pain and suffer and that they are subordinate to men, precluding their participation in the priesthood.

For nearly sixteen hundred years, Mother Mary was placed in juxtaposition to Mary Magdalene misrepresented as a penitent whore. The 1969 declaration exonerating Magdalene had little fanfare and brought minimal change in liturgy. The fulcra of women's roles in Christianity had been construed as extremes, virgin and whore, for so long. It appeared that the Church didn't want Christian women to have real role models. Ironically, many people were unaware of Magdalene's official change of status until they read Dan Brown's novel, *The DaVinci Code.*

During the earliest days of Christianity many groups competed for the legitimacy of their recollections and beliefs, which would frame the basis of the fledgling religion. Disciples, "pupils" and followers of Christ, were often at odds when accounting for details of Jesus' life and teaching, especially after time passed and memories clouded. The real battle, however, was the argument regarding apostolic authority—that is, specifying which followers are authorized to teach and preach the word of God.

To help us consider the issue of apostolic authority, let's first ask: What is an apostle? How do we define apostolic mission?

Apparently there is no definitive answer to which scholars can agree. There are several descriptions, however, that seem to satisfy many. According to wordnet.Princeton.edu, apostle means:

- An ardent early supporter of a cause or reform; "an apostle of a revolution"

- Any important early teacher of Christianity or a Christian missionary to a people

- One of the original twelve disciples chosen by Christ to preach his gospel (New Testament).

Ann Graham Brock opens our eyes to a deeper perspective on this issue in her highly informative book, *Mary Magdalene, The First Apostle: The Struggle for Authority.* Among the controversies and contradictions through the centuries within the Christian Church regarding apostolic authority, Brock distinguishes between Pauline and Petrine definitions. Saint Paul justifies his status as apostle both as a witness to Christ's Resurrection and as a calling to proclaim Christ's message (Brock, p. 6). Although not present at the time of the resurrection, Paul's claimed status as apostolic witness is based on the resurrection appearances made to him by the Risen Christ. Paul is willing to extend that status to others who have also witnessed the resurrected Christ as well as to those for whom others vouched. From those names he assembles a lengthy list (Brock, p. 10). But the "official list" of apostles became exclusively the twelve males named by the author of Luke, perhaps as some have said to avoid the critics of women predominant among Romans of the day. Peter, who was aggrandized by Luke, became the spokesman of the "official apostles" (Brock, p. 45). As Brock points out, "apostles" and "the twelve" apparently did not become synonymous until after the time of Paul, thanks in great measure to the author of Luke (Brock, pp. 11, 154). As a consequence of identifying "the twelve" as *the* "apostles," the author of Luke (and likely "Acts" as well) excludes female leaders and female apostles (especially Mary Magdalene) of early Christianity along with Paul and James, the brother of Jesus who would ultimately head the Jerusalem church (Brock, p. 151).

Gregory of Antioch, a contemporary of Pope Gregory, proclaimed in the sixth century that when Jesus approached "Mary Magdalene and the other Mary" at the tomb, he said, "Be the first teachers to the teachers. So that Peter who denied me learns that I can also choose women as apostles" (Brock, p. 15; also <http://www.womenpriests.org/magdala/index.asp>). That statement would seem to support the case for women's claim to apostolic authority. But other forces came into play over time.

Brock insists that the marginalizing of women's roles in the early church was calculated and deliberate, reflecting the mores of the times. Eliminating women from consideration as "apostle" in particular was as simple as discrediting the candidate or changing the definition. Several gospels supplied the ammunition, especially when interpreted by a patriarchal hierarchy. There was an overt struggle for authority, according to Brock, between Peter and Mary Magdalene. We know how the struggle played out, but why?

The author of Luke gave credence to the Petrine approach. Unlike the author of John, who credits Mary Magdalene as the first witness to the Resurrection charged with telling the others (John 20:17), Luke's author elevates the role of Peter making him the first "credible" witness (Luke 24:1-12). This happens only in Luke, usually portraying women in secondary roles with behavior stereotypical for the time: prayerful, quiet, and supportive of male leadership (Brock, p. 37). Matthew and Mark's gospels were closer to John in content than to Luke. In Luke we see information added that is not in other gospels; information unflattering to Peter is ignored; existing information is altered to portray him more favorably. The author of Luke plays an instrumental role in undermining and diminishing female roles while positively spinning the leadership of Peter. The Gospel of Peter echoes the intent and content of Luke. Both deny Mary Magdalene as a witness who has been commissioned to share the good news. Manipulation of information and spin in Luke clearly presents a much different scenario than in most other gospels.

Brock goes on to underscore the significance of the Nag Hammadi texts and their new information and insights that shed further light on the power struggle between Peter and Mary Magdalene. The codices reflect the diversity of opinion even during the early days of Christianity. Individuals highlighted represent the author's loyalties and perspectives. According to Brock, most narratives describing the resurrection accounts are very similar but may differ with respect to those who were named as witnesses. She illustrates this by noting that Syriac and Coptic texts depict Mother Mary rather than Mary Magdalene conversing with Jesus in the garden as the first resurrection appearance (p. 18).

Adding to the discrepancies in gospels, we see an obvious contrast between the Acts of Paul and the Acts of Peter. In Pauline apostleship there is a definite association with strong female leadership; Petrine apostleship makes no such connection. Paul's Acts credits Thecla in particular, along with Eubula, Artemella, and many other women, strengthening and commissioning them. Paul says to Thecla, "Go and teach the word of God!" Some feel that women's actions as represented in Paul's Acts helped raise the prestige of Apostle Paul rather than improve women's status. In other words, women were his character witnesses. Paul was not, after all, one of the "original twelve." In Acts of Peter, we observe that no women give speeches of encouragement to anyone (Brock, p. 108). Perhaps as Brock points out Peter was selected as a "figure of choice for voicing objections to women's leadership status" (p. 104).

Displacing the Leadership of Mary Magdalene

There are many who feel that the figure of Mary Magdalene was deliberately dissociated from her role as witness and apostle. As indicated earlier, the two methods used for accomplishing that goal were to discredit her and to redefine "apostle."

Conflation with the prostitute on the one hand and conflation with Mother Mary helped accomplish the confusion. (There were those who chose to further marginalize Mary Magdalene by ascribing some of her actions to

Mother Mary, who better represented their approved role of women.) Why did they feel the need to make such deliberate changes? Was it because they feared that critics of Christianity would discount the word of a woman as the fledgling movement struggled to expand? Or was it something more insidious such as maintaining the ideals of patriarchy, ignoring the example of Jesus who considered women as equals?

Karen King, a renowned biblical scholar, asserts that the configuration of the movement following Jesus' death was not an established church with a clear organizational structure. The structure evolved over time out of a variety of possibilities into "the patriarchal and hierarchal structure still extant today." In an excerpt of The Gospel of Mary featured in Dan Burstein's book *Secrets of Mary Magdalene*, King talks about the various formats ranging from a loosely structured charismatic group to a highly formal and fixed organization (p. 103). She says that some congregations shared leadership among men and women, inspired by the Spirit movement that stressed the gifts of prophecy, teaching, healing, administration, and service. Other groups, more formal in varying degrees, featured the leadership of elders, bishops, deacons, and widows. Many Christian sects welcomed women and slaves in significant leadership roles; others held to the traditional social order excluding then. When the original Gospel of Mary was written, the church organization was still unclear (p. 103).

King also argues that The Gospel of Mary disputes apostolic authority as it came to be interpreted. Authority should be based on "understanding and appropriating the gospel" rather than "solely or primarily on a succession of past witnesses." She says authority should be determined in the leadership of both men and women "who have attained strength of character and spiritual maturity" (p. 104).

Susan Haskins, author of *Mary Magdalene: Myth and Metaphor,* also describes the Christian movement during the first twenty to thirty years following Jesus' death as very attractive to women since it was liberating and welcoming to them. This information was corroborated, according to Haskins, by Celsus, a pagan writer of the second century who mocked Christianity as "a religion of women capable only of appealing to the simple and lowly and those without understanding such as women, slaves and children." He further jeers that the Resurrection itself "had been based on reports of hysterical women" (p. 85). This kind of criticism, along with an inherent problem with female leadership among Church fathers, fueled the actions yet to come. Celsus' anti-woman comments, however, support the modern assertions of significant involvement of women in the emerging Church.

As previously asserted, modern scholarship has determined that Mary Magdalene was indeed considered a leader by many in the early days of the Christian movement. The so-called Gnostic texts reveal that Magdalene was the topic of much discussion and a figure to be reckoned with. Most women of the day were identified by their relationship with a close male relative—such as daughter of Peter, wife of Clopas, etc. In Hebraic genealogy, daughters did not have the same value as sons and men were supposedly the "owners of the name."

Some women, however, were identified by their place of birth, such as Mary of Nazareth and Mary of Magdala. The fact that she is identified by her town of Magdala rather than by her husband or son tells us that she had value beyond her association with a male. Furthermore, the fact that her apostolic authority is discussed in many if not most gospels, whether orthodox or Gnostic, indicates that she is a significant player.

In his introduction to *Secrets of Mary Magdalene*, Dan Burstein notes that all the sources revering Mary Magdalene as leader were excluded from the New Testament canon (p. 5). The message conveyed in this selection was intended to exclude women from participating in Church leadership.

Some critics of feminist interpretations accuse their authors of attempting to "rewrite history." Indeed these authors do bring a different spin and different agenda, but their intent is to revise what has been claimed as "history" for millennia in order to present a more truthful picture of what actually happened. Burstein underscores the fact that *every one* of the discovered codices mentions Mary Magdalene. He indicates further that the Gospel of Mary Magdalene, the Gospel of Thomas, the Gospel of Philip, the Wisdom of Faith, and the Dialogue of the Savior "unanimously picture Mary Magdalene as one of Jesus' most trusted disciples" (p. 3). Some even refer to Magdalene as Jesus' most trusted confidant and the one capable of understanding his deepest secrets.

The Gospel of Mary and the Gospel of Thomas, for example, both speak of the leadership struggles between Magdalene and Peter. In the former,

Peter challenges Magdalene's reliability to represent the master's words. He does not believe that Jesus would trust Magdalene, a woman, with secrets he had not shared with the male disciples. Levi ends the dispute by supporting Magdalene. Accusing Peter of being a hothead, Levi says to him, "If the Savior made her worthy, who are you to reject her . . ." In the latter, Peter also opposes the role of women among the disciples but here he is rebuked by Jesus who firmly establishes their role. As Burstein points out (p. 4) both those gospels were probably written ca. 90–100 CE, when the question of women as disciples was igniting firestorms of disagreements among followers.

In a June 2006 article in *Smithsonian*, James Carroll claims that before the gospel accounts were classified as "The New Testament," "Jesus rejection of the prevailing male dominance was being eroded in the Christian Community." He reminds us that the gospels were documenting memories influenced by numerous theological perspectives rather than recording historical facts. Since they were written thirty-five to sixty-five years after the death of Jesus, they cannot be perceived as "eye-witness accounts" according to Carroll. Mary Magdalene, he says, was discredited not just because of her gender; her rejection was also a rebuke of sexuality in general. Carroll cites a Susan Haskins summary in an article in Burstein's *Secrets of Mary Magdalene* which says, "[Magdalene was presented as] the redeemed whore and Christianity's model of repentance, a manageable and controllable figure, and an effective weapon and instrument of propaganda against her own sex" (p. 36). Carroll adds that the "myth" focused on the possibility of forgiveness and redemption, "but what drove the anti-sexual sexualizing of Mary Magdalene was the male need to dominate women."

The approved gospels emphasized the "authority of the twelve," providing the underlying rationale for exclusion of women from the priesthood. There are many who feel that Magdalene's distortion was a manipulation by males who succeeded for centuries in keeping females in their "proper places." Eve was a scapegoat for the Fall of Man, and Mary Magdalene—by association—carried her torch forward.

In the Roundtable chapter of *Secrets of Mary Magdalene*, Susan Haskins provides a timeline to help us understand the metamorphosis of Magdalene's image (p. 187) telling us that her image began to change even during the early period of Christianity. We already mentioned that there were people who chose to discredit the role of women, considering them unreliable and hysterical. Those denigrating Magdalene would need to take special care in discreetly labeling the woman acknowledged as the primary witness to the risen Christ in three of the four canonized gospels. As we have said before, the strategy was to validate the act of witness while diminishing the stature of the woman.

As the Christian fathers struggled to sort out the many Marys, Gregory the Great conflated them in 591 and "settled" the discussion. Equating Mary Magdalene with a prostitute made her endearingly "human" to her followers but became especially damaging to her leadership image as greater emphasis was being placed on celibacy in the Church. Other related issues also emerged in Church dogma such as marriage for priests which was forbidden by doctrine in 1100, the concept of Mother Mary's virginity, the significance of penance, and the divinity of Christ as supported by Mary's virginity. Formalized Church doctrine and dogma became even more rigorous and by 1215 the Sacrament of Penance was established requiring that all Christians go to church, make confessions, and take communion.

As a result of all those changes in philosophy, theology, and dogma, Haskins contends, Mary Magdalene's persona—formerly perceived as the symbol of penance and communion—changed to one of lust with all its negative connotation. "Sermons about her referenced lust, vanity, and her worldly life" (p. 188). Mary Magdalene's significance as first witness and courageous apostle to the apostles was thus lost to a distorted misrepresentation of fact.

Elaine Pagels contends that the traditional church has depicted Mary Magdalene as a prostitute, whereas modern interpretations depict her as a wife and lover of Jesus. Both, she says, reduce her to a sexual image. But sexuality is only one aspect of one's persona. It is time to emphasize other attributes of Magdalene such as her courage, spirituality, independence, leadership, intelligence, and communication skills.

There is a strange irony in the enthusiasm of those preferring to believe Mary Magdalene was a penitent whore rather than a charismatic, visionary, independent woman and early church leader. Joan Acocella feels that people cling to the whore representation because "it made her human and gave them hope, since even a prostitute could get to heaven" ("The Saintly Sinner" in *The*

New Yorker, February 13, 2006). Mary Magdalene was, after all, the patron saint of prostitutes, barrel makers, and gardeners along with glove makers, perfume makers, and hairdressers who provided the accoutrements of the oldest profession, says Acocella. They were the common folk who identified with her, or at least with her contrived reputation. People were attracted to her passion and fervor as well as her perceived vulnerability. Perhaps they felt that by losing her tarnish, Magdalene had lost her mettle.

One of the descriptions of Mary Magdalene that most resonates with my own spiritual convictions is that of Kathleen McGowan (Burstein, p. 289). She describes Magdalene's message as "one of love, tolerance, and forgiveness and personal accountability." McGowan says Magdalene sends a message of unity and non-judgment for all people of all belief systems. Her sexuality, or lack of it, should be irrelevant, in my opinion.

Even if we use only the sanctioned gospel passages as references, we can conclude that both Mother Mary, a.k.a. Blessed Virgin Mary, and Mary Magdalene were clearly courageous, loyal, and close to Jesus, having heard first-hand the lessons of his teaching. Given what we are learning from new interpretations of other versions of gospels, there are indications that they were much more than that, as teachers and evangelists sharing the good news of their beloved. Mother Mary surely did not live out her years at Ephesus in silence.

Finally, Susan Haskins says that because of her association with sexuality, Mary Magdalene "has come to represent the liberated woman of the late 20th century and her myth has been recreated in that light: she is a rebel, a traveler, an independent woman; she might even have a child by Christ" (*Mary Magdalene: Myth and Metaphor*, p. 383). Believe what you will about her maternity, but Mary Magdalene continues to inspire vast numbers of women of the twenty-first century as more and more information is revealed about her accomplishments and leadership.

Despite the modern evidence that many women did indeed play instrumental roles in the formulation of the early Christian movement and assumed leadership roles for at least several centuries, the Vatican seems determined to cling to the old ways. Haskins references Pope John Paul II's second encyclical "Mulieris Dignitatem" ("On the Dignity and Vocation of Women"). There he appears to say that men and women are equal, to acknowledge women's

special role in Christian history, to denounce some of the early condemna-
tions, and to sing their praises. He draws the line at ordination, however, citing Christ's calling as apostles to men only. So there we are. Current Vatican
indicators are no more encouraging.

Under the helm of Pope Benedict, women's "attempted ordination" has
resulted in the excommunication of the women who were ordained, along
with the male priests who performed the ordinations. Further, in July 2010,
as the Vatican was updating 2001 norms dealing with "priestly abuse of
minors," they included "attempted women's ordination" as a "delicta graviora," one of the most serious crimes against the Church (July 9, 2010
<http://www.catholicnews.com/data/stories/cns/1002793.htm>). Delicta
graviora cases are reserved for the Congregation for the Doctrine of the
Faith, over which Cardinal Joseph Ratzinger, now Pope Benedict, presided
for twenty-three years.

Needless to say, the blogosphere erupted with emotional comments.
According to Bryan Cones, U.S. Catholic editor, ". . . it is an outrage to pair
the two [sex abuse of children and women's ordinations], a complete injustice
to connect the aspirations of some women among the baptized to ordained
ministry with what are some of the worst crimes that can be committed
against the least of Christ's members." Cones goes on to say that the move
is a mistake, plain and simple, imprudent at best; at worst a serious blow to
Rome's already damaged credibility (July 9, 2010 <http://www.uscatholic.
org/blog/2010/07/sex-abuse-and-womens-ordination>).

On April 14, 2009, Thomas C. Fox reported, in an article in the *National
Catholic Reporter,* that the Vatican's Congregation for the Doctrine of the Faith
recently had begun investigating the Leadership Conference of Women Religious, the largest U.S. women's religious leadership organization. At issue in
this unfortunately continuing "doctrinal investigation" is the group's alleged
objectionable stand on ordination to the priesthood, attitudes towards non-
Catholics and "the problem of homosexuality" (http://ncronline.org/news/
women/vatican-investigates-us-women-religious-leadership).

None of this bodes well for the status of women in the Catholic Church.

5

Ballot Boxes, Burning Bras, and the Pill

So far, we have been discussing long-ago and far-away historical issues that have affected the status of women. We've been examining the building blocks and "rationale" for misogyny, which often seem connected to the onus placed on Eve for her transgression. In this chapter we explore highlights of the development of women's rights in the United States from the middle of the nineteenth century until recent years.

We will attempt to address these questions:

- Why did it take so long and what were the obstacles?
- What is the status of the Equal Rights Amendment and why has it never been ratified?
- What were the impacts of the "Pink Collar Ghetto" and the "Glass Ceiling" on upward mobility opportunities for women?
- Is today's younger generation of women aware of the struggles and sacrifices made by their "sisters"?
- Are women losing ground in this decade because of their perceived detachment?
- Many people feel that women have come a long way in achieving equal partnership with men, but what challenges remain?
- Does the subconscious association of women with Eve remain in our cellular memory and influence attitudes and decisions made by organizations?
- Do patriarchal organizations have the clout they once did?

The Struggle for Women's Suffrage

If you ask when the Women's Rights Movement began, most people will cite the 1960s. In reality, the Women's Movement began in 1848. On July 13 of that year, at a summer tea party in Seneca Falls, New York, Elizabeth Cady Stanton and four of her friends discussed the status of women of the era. Stanton was frustrated that despite the roles women had played in helping patriots win independence from tyranny, they were not afforded the same rights and privileges as men. Within several days of the tea and conversation, these women of action planned a convention to take up this issue. They set a date, place, and agenda to "discuss the social, civil, and religious condition and rights of woman." This public meeting at the Wesleyan Chapel in Seneca Falls on July 19 and 20 made history as the apparent first of its type in western civilization.

Using the Declaration of Independence as a model, Elizabeth crafted a "Declaration of Sentiments" enumerating grievances of women: the lack of voting rights or property rights, the requirement to pay property taxes without the right to vote, exclusion from educational opportunities, limited employment opportunities and huge pay discrepancies, and more. She also stated that in most cases women were denied participation in Church affairs. Admittedly, enslaved Black women fared even worse. Stanton was optimistic, however, that she and her supporters could influence those in power while the republic was still young.

At the first convention, attendees unanimously passed the Declaration of Sentiments and twelve resolutions. The only resolution that met with resistance was the one enfranchising the female vote. Many women questioned the need to vote, claiming that their husbands took care of that. It was Frederick Douglas who argued, "Suffrage is the power to choose leaders and make laws, and the right by which all others are secured." The resolution succeeded with a scant majority.

Stanton's wish that this convention would be followed by many others was fulfilled: Women's Rights conventions were held regularly from 1850 until their interruption by the Civil War. She was joined early on by other activists including Susan B. Anthony, Matilda Joslyn Gage, and Lucy Stone, the movement's pioneer theoreticians. But the backlash and negative responses she anticipated also came to fruition, as we shall discuss.

Matilda Joslyn Gage

Elizabeth Cady Stanton and Susan B. Anthony are familiar names in the struggle for women's suffrage. A name less familiar is Matilda Joslyn Gage, to whom we frequently referred in Chapter 3.

The words on her tombstone sum up the passion she felt for her life's work: *There is a word sweeter than Mother, Home or Heaven, that word is Liberty.*

Born in 1826 just outside Syracuse, New York, Matilda was exposed to social issues early on, living in an abolitionist home that served as a station on the Underground Railroad. She played a major role in the early movement which was later diminished because of her perceived radical positions—especially with respect to the Church at a time when the support of the Women's Christian Temperance Union (WCTU) was needed for suffrage success. Gage was adamant about the need to maintain separation of church and state, whereas the WCTU supported elimination of that concept. She bristled at the thought of their proposed amendment to the U.S. Constitution naming Christ as the author and head of the American government. Gage expressed her disgust with what she called "a return to Middle Ages and proscription for religious opinions" and saw as a move away from the goals of women's true freedom (http://www.matildajoslyngage.org/gage-home/religious-freedom-room/). Her refusal to cooperate with the WCTU caused a rift between her and Stanton, who felt Matilda was jeopardizing the success of the Suffrage Movement.

Gage's uncredited work on *The Woman's Bible* with Elizabeth Cady Stanton and her own book *Woman, Church and State* were decades ahead of their time.

Revolution and the Battles for Equality

It should come as no surprise that women's suffrage had many detractors. The anti-suffrage-for-women people, or "antis" as they were called, attacked the intellectual capabilities of women claiming they were inferior to men. How could women possibly make an intelligent decision about candidates?

The "weaker sex" could not handle the stress of an election, according to their thinking. The opposition also targeted female emotions, claiming that women's emotional instability would cloud their judgment and make them dangerous voters. The fear-based arguments of the antis preached that allowing women to vote would threaten national security and would lead to morality issues.

Misogynists warned that suffrage would result in "a shifting of gender roles, producing a nation of transvestites." H.W. Frink, a New York psychologist, summed up his opinion of feminists in 1918, stating, "A certain proportion of at least the most militant suffragists are neurotics who in some instances are compensating for masculine trends, in others, are more or less successfully sublimating sadistic and homosexual ones" (http://www.history. rochester.edu/class/suffrage/home.htm). Women, in their view, were trying to be like men and they condemned the demand by activists who "want the vote and we want it when we want it!" One anti speaking at a hearing in Connecticut retorted, "That is the old story—of woman—Eve. She got it and we've had trouble ever since" (http://www.history.rochester.edu/class/ suffrage/Anti.html)

Not all antis were men and not all supporters were women, however. The movement had male supporters among its ranks and there were also women opposed to suffrage. In fact, in 1911 The National Association Opposed to Women Suffrage (NAOWS) was initiated under the leadership of Mrs. Arthur Dodge. According to an online compilation of suffrage milestones, this group included wealthy women and some Catholic clergymen. Distillers and brewers, as well as "urban political machines, Southern congressmen, and corporate capitalists—like railroad magnates and meatpackers" discreetly funded NAOWS' campaign (http://lcweb2.loc.gov/ammem/naw/nawstime.html). Some of the angst came from those fearing the association of the Women's Christian Temperance Union with the suffragists. The WCTU, founded in 1874, had become an active ally with the suffrage movement. The antis felt the women's vote would be aggressively used against the sale of liquor. This fear actually came to fruition. The National Prohibition Act, also called the Volstead Act, was in effect from 1920–1933 as the 18th Amendment until it was superseded by the 21st Amendment that gives states their own determination rights. The manufacture, transportation, import, export, and sale of alcoholic beverages were prohibited during that period.

An amendment for Women's Suffrage was finally introduced in the United States Congress in 1878, but it did not pass both houses until 1919. Thirty-six states were needed to ratify the amendment, and the battle lines were drawn in Tennessee which was poised to become the thirty-sixth state. It is said that Harry Burn, a twenty-four-year-old Tennessee legislator, had voted with the antis all along, but with a vote projected to be 48 to 48, he took his mother's advice and voted in favor of the Suffrage Amendment. As a result, Tennessee provided the deciding vote for ratification as the thirty-sixth state, and The Women's Suffrage Amendment was ratified as the 19th Amendment on August 26, 1920.

Some credit the success with the good will created by the hiatus suffragists took during World War I to assist in the war effort by working in factories. To some, that work certainly underscored that the vote for women was deserved. The National Women's Party under the leadership of Alice Paul and her eight thousand marchers had gotten President Woodrow Wilson's attention during his first inauguration, followed by further action at his second. But after the War, Carrie Chapman Catt, representing the so-called less aggressive National American Woman Suffrage Association, persisted in convincing President Wilson that the women's work during the war deserved the reward of women's suffrage. In a change of heart, he reputedly said on September 18, 1918: "We have made partners of the women in this war. Shall we admit them only to a partnership of suffering and sacrifice and toil and not to a partnership of right?"

Faced with powerful antagonists, The Women's Suffrage campaign had taken seventy-two years!

Although a majority of those who did battle in the organized Women's Rights Movement went their separate ways, satisfied with the right to vote, a few like Alice Paul knew that the fight for women's rights was not over. In 1923 she outlined her rendition of an Equal Rights Amendment for the U.S. Constitution that would guarantee equal rights for men and women regardless of where they live in this country. In addition, around the time of Suffrage success, Margaret Sanger, a public health nurse, raised the issue of birth control, an area which had not been incorporated into the Declaration of Sentiments. This movement questioned the viability of women's emancipation if they did not have control over their own bodies. They supported education about known birth control options. As you might expect, this group met with zealous opposition, which we will discuss later.

Women's Rights: Phase Two

The 1960s were marked by an unpopular war, civil rights actions, campus unrest, distrust of authority, and an awakening of sexual freedom and "free love" precipitated by development of "the pill." We acknowledge this period as the emergence of Phase Two of the Women's Movement, decades after the success of Women's Suffrage and more than a century after the pioneers began the battle.

The colorful sixties and seventies were decades of challenge, change, violence, beatniks and "peaceniks." While "draft dodgers" burned their draft cards in protest of what they called an unjust war, feminists were reputed to be burning their bras in symbolic protest of sexism and perceived trivialization of the revitalized women's movement. There is some dispute as to whether the "bra burning" is truth or a myth used to bring attention to the movement. Feminist activists equated objects (like bras) as symbols of patriarchal oppression and ridiculed their need. What likely happened, chroniclers say, is that many women chose not to wear bras and left them home rather than publicly burning them.

The "myth" may have found its roots in the 1968 protest against the Miss America Pageant which some viewed as an oppression of women. Several hundred women from New York Radical Women protested the pageant, criticizing the "ludicrous standards of beauty" and the hypocrisy of a double Madonna-whore fantasy imposed on women. " They filled a "Freedom Trash Can" with some bras, high-heeled shoes, girdles, curlers, *Playboy* magazines, etc., deemed to be " items of oppression." According to some reports, women tried to secure a permit to set the items on fire but were refused because of the potential hazard to the wooden boardwalk of Atlantic City (http://womenshistory.about.com/od/feminism/a/miss_america_protest.htm).

The stuff legends are made of!

Events of these two decades underscored the need to renew women's rights efforts. Esther Peterson, director of the Women's Bureau of the Department of Labor in 1961, encouraged President Kennedy to investigate discrimination against women. In response he named Eleanor Roosevelt as chair of a newly formed Commission on the Status of Women. Research data indicated that women were victims of discrimination in nearly every aspect of their lives. State and local governments replicated the concept, forming their own commissions to study regional circumstances and to recommend changes.

In addition, employment discrimination based on sex, race, religion, and national origin were forbidden by the passage of Title VII of the 1964 Civil Rights Act. (Some feel that the word "sex" was added as a last minute attempt to derail the Act.) The Equal Employment Opportunity Commission was established, followed by the creation of the National Organization for Women, frustrated that fifty thousand filed sex discrimination complaints were not being pursued. In addition, many women were involved with anti-war and civil rights activities on college campuses across the country. New legions of activist women had been ignited.

Among other trigger events for the resurgence of the Women's Movement was the publication of Betty Friedan's book, *The Feminine Mystique*, in 1963 exposing "emotional and intellectual oppression" of middle-class women who had "limited life options." According to Friedan, "A woman has got to be able to say, and not feel guilty, 'Who am I, and what do I want out of my life?' She mustn't feel selfish and neurotic if she wants goals of her own, outside of her husband and children" (http://www.usatoday.com/news/nation/2006-02-04-friedan-obit_x.htm). Friedan, who was a founder and first president of the National Organization for Women, supported controversial issues of the time such as abortion, equal pay, maternity leave, upward mobility for women, etc. But she was significantly more mainstream than her more radical sisters, advising women to consider men as allies rather than enemies and to avoid rejecting the family. She ultimately left NOW as it moved in a direction with which she was uncomfortable.

Also during the 1960s the Rand Corporation was commissioned to conduct a Delphi Study using expert panels to forecast a world population that was growing exponentially. During the process it was determined that a contraceptive "pill" would dramatically impact that projected population growth. Although the word sex always evokes an emotional response, whether good or bad, it became the focus of discussion and action.

Sexual Revolution

The Victorian era, viewed as a period of sexual repression and prudishness, ended in 1901; but U.S. sexual attitudes were held hostage by Victorian principles for many decades later. Fear and guilt were key ingredients once again. Women were not allowed to enjoy sex for fear of contributing to moral decline. After all, a woman's value prior to marriage was predicated on her chastity and virtue, and finding a suitable husband would be difficult if she were considered "loose."

A predominant view espoused in 1888 by William Acton in *Functions and Disorders of the Reproductive Organs* claimed that women experienced no need for sex and that they were generally apathetic to the idea of sex in marriage. According to John S. and Robin M. Haller in their book *The Physician and Sexuality in Victorian America*, Dr. Mary Wood Allen (superintendent of the Purity Department of the Women's Christian Temperance Union) believed that "the most genuine love between husband and wife existed in the lofty sphere of the platonic embrace." Elizabeth Blackwell, a physician of the period, believed that women's disinterest in sexual passion was the result of fear of injury from childbirth. A medical journal, *The Alkaloidal Clinic*, claimed in 1891 that lack of women's education contributed to their belief that sexual feeling was "indecent and immoral" (http://www.cwrl.utexas.edu/~ulrich/femhist/sexuality.shtml).

Given our Puritanical roots and strong Victorian influences, it is no wonder that women struggled with their sexuality. Prior to marriage, sexual activity was unheard of for women with "proper" values, although men were assumed to have lost their virginity. Before marriage, women feared the "loose" label along with the possibility of pregnancy. After marriage, women had little incentive to be sexually engaged since sex was male-dominated and unfulfilling for women. Furthermore, conjugal acts were only supposed to be performed as necessary for procreation or as her wifely "duty." Ultimately, many long held beliefs would come apart as social attitudes and mores were transformed.

Finally, the 1960s and 70s exploded into a sexual revolution promoted by a counter-culture that questioned authority, materialism, and many political and cultural norms. Steamy novels and Hollywood X-rated films accelerated a voyeurism that enhanced the sexual mentality. Embracing the ideals of peace, love, and harmony, young people attempted to expand their awareness through psychedelic drugs, mysticism, and yoga. "Free love" was indulged by many thousands of young people who touted the power of love and the beauty of sex as an entitlement of college life. Their lifestyles nearly eliminated former inhibitions imposed by old Victorian standards. Unprotected sex had its consequences, of course, so the advent of greater choices of contraceptives in the opinion of many provided freedom for women wishing to enjoy the pleasures of sex without its potential complications.

Margaret Sanger had long been an advocate for birth control, and had opened the first birth control clinic in the United States in Brooklyn, New York, in 1916. She and her sister Ethel Byrne worked to chip away at the Comstock Act, which prohibited the use of the mail system to "transmit obscene materials or articles addressing or for use in the prevention of conception, including information on birth control methods or birth control devices themselves." The Comstock Act, also known as the *Act for Suppression of Trade in and Circulation of Obscene Literature and Articles of Immoral Use,* was passed by Congress in 1873 as a result of efforts by temperance unions and anti-vice societies to prohibit birth control devices.

Sanger and Byrne spent thirty days in a workhouse for violating the Comstock Act. Many states had laws banning sale, distribution, and advertising of contraceptives; but Connecticut actually had a law banning their use. Apparently no thought had been given to the enforceability of the law. In 1916 Sanger's associate Mary Ware Dennett initiated the National Birth Control League, which Sanger directed and renamed Planned Parenthood Organization in 1942. Sanger was also responsible in part for the overturn of Connecticut's restrictive law in the case of Griswold v. Connecticut, a statute that allowed police officers to search homes for evidence of contraception. Such actions ultimately were held to be unconstitutional, violating the right to marital privacy.

The United States v. One Package decision in 1936 struck down the Comstock Act's classification of birth control literature as obscene. Then the Supreme Court decision in 1964 overturning Griswold v. Connecticut served to articulate the constitutional "right to privacy." This decision was later interpreted as the basis for the right of unmarried persons to use birth control in Eisenstadt v. Baird (1972) and ultimately the right to terminate pregnancies in the 1973 Roe v. Wade decision.

Underscoring the significance of Supreme Court actions, we now know that as a result of a series of legislations, contraceptives were considered legal for married couples in all states by 1965 and were finally approved for singles in 1972. Surely the production of contraceptives, including "the pill," and their easy accessibility contributed to the proliferation of sex during that time. But tempering this accessibility was the guilt imposed on Catholics by a 1930 encyclical by Pope Pius IX calling birth control, by any means, a sin. Legality conflicted with Church "morality."

In contrast, earlier that year, the Lambeth Conference of Anglican Bishops approved a resolution allowing limited acceptance of birth control. By 1961, the National Council of Churches supported a liberal policy toward birth control, pending mutual agreement of couples. In 1968, however, Pope Paul VI affirmed the 1930 document of Pius IX with his own encyclical, *Humanae Vitae*, which stands today as official Church doctrine. The encyclical bases its rationale on the natural law of Aristotle, Augustine, and Aquinas stating that procreation is the end purpose of sexuality; to alter that natural process violates natural law and is a sin. This view is also supported by Evangelicals, Christian fundamentalists, and some Anglicans (Kathleen O'Grady, *Contraception and Religion*, p. 2 <http://mum.org/contraception>).

Free love and rampant sex came to a screeching halt during the mid-1980s as the deadly AIDS epidemic, sexually transmitted, was revealed. Instead of asking "What's your Sun sign?" prospective daters were more interested in sexual history and whether or not he/she had been tested for AIDS (Acquired Immune Disease Syndrome). It was the proverbial "rude awakening"!! Considered by some as a pandemic responsible for more than twenty-five million deaths, there is still no known vaccine or cure.

The Equal Rights Amendment Revisited

The National Women's Party introduced the Equal Rights Amendment in 1923 but it lay dormant for fifty years. The Amendment simply stated, *"Equality of rights under the law shall not be denied or abridged by the United States or by any state on account of sex."* Congress ultimately passed the Amendment in 1972 and forwarded it to the states for ratification. Women confident of winning the thirty-eight states needed for ratification mobilized their ranks, marching, canvassing, and increasing awareness as they sought financial support for their efforts to accomplish ratification. Women from all backgrounds and economic strata participated in the national campaign and women's rights organizations thrived.

But they had not anticipated the backlash and opposition. They also had not anticipated the effectiveness of Phyllis Schlafly and her supporters, who feared that ratification would sanction greater government control over personal lives. They pointed to the onset of unisex bathrooms, decline of families, drafting of women into military, and other such claims. Although there was clear support among women in state legislatures for ratification, there were not enough women legislators. Furthermore, politicians considered the bill controversial and only 46 percent of them voted for ratification. The vote was three states short of ratification when the deadline arrived ten years later in 1982.

There seems to be a lot of mystery about what the Equal Rights Amendment actually said, but rather it was the "spin" that provoked the angst. The entire amendment is worded as follows:

The Equal Rights Amendment

- Section 1. Equality of rights under the law shall not be denied or abridged by the United States or by any state on account of sex.

- Section 2. The Congress shall have the power to enforce, by appropriate legislation, the provisions of this article.

- Section 3. This amendment shall take effect two years after the date of ratification.

The Equal Rights Amendment has been reintroduced numerous times, but opponents challenge that earlier state ratifications are no longer valid. During the 110th Congress (2007–2008) Senator Edward Kennedy acted as lead sponsor for a reintroduction of the ERA as S.J. Res. 10, and Representative Carolyn Maloney of New York was lead sponsor of H.J. Res. 40. Neither bill imposes a deadline on the ratification process. These bills are of course supported by women's organizations. They encourage others to advocate for the bill and seek additional co-sponsors. The ERA Bill has not yet been taken up by the 111th Congress, although Rep. Carolyn Maloney D-NY and Rep. Judy Biggert R-IL, along with seventy-seven co-sponsors proposed an ERA resolution (H.J. Res. 61) in October 2009. The Bill was referred to the Subcommittee on the Constitution, Civil Rights and Civil Liberties. Unfortunately such bills often stay in committee and, with no current momentum, it would appear that for the time being the Equal Rights Amendment is in limbo. How ironic.

The fifteen states which have not yet ratified the ERA are: Alabama, Arizona, Arkansas, Florida, Georgia, Illinois, Louisiana, Mississippi, Missouri, Nevada, North Carolina, Oklahoma, South Carolina, Utah, and Virginia. Only three more states are needed for ratification.

Title IX of the Educational Amendments of 1972

Title IX emerged around the time of ERA passage in Congress and simply states, "No person in the United States shall, on the basis of sex, be excluded from participation in, be denied benefits of, or be subjected to discrimination under any education program or activity receiving Federal financial assistance." Enacted on June 23, 1972, the act affected high school and collegiate athletic activities, although it was intended to encompass ALL academic activities including accessibility to all academic fields including math and science. The American Association of University Women applauds the concept of the act but questions the effectiveness of government enforcement. Violations went unnoticed and many schools failed to comply with guidelines.

Title IX has been credited with opening doors for female athletes through development of women's professional sports. It has been under attack, however, by those claiming that some schools have had to eliminate traditional male programs since budgets can't accommodate both. Supporters of Title IX counter that "non-revenue" sports were being cancelled even before passage of Title IX and furthermore that GAO (Government Accountability Office) statistics indicate that male collegiate sport participation has increased since inception of Title IX. The attack was carried out as well by a Bush administration policy issued by the Department of Education with no public notice or input. The "clarification" allowed schools to comply by sending female students email surveys inquiring about their ability to play additional sports. Failure to reply may be interpreted as disinterest. Prior to this clarification, more vigorous efforts were required to gauge interest. This seemed to be a back door approach to weakening the spirit and intent of the law, a tactic being used against other existing laws protecting the interests of women.

In April, 2010, the Obama administration reversed the previous administration's policy of allowing electronic surveys to demonstrate "full" compliance with Title IX. Colleges must now ensure that male and female participation is directly proportionate to their student enrollment numbers. They also have to prove that they have been responsive to students' developing interests and abilities or indicate in other ways that they are recognizing and accommodating the interests of female athletes (http://www.collegenews.com/index. php?/article/obama_administration_facelieft_of_title_ix_sparks_praise_ protests_0421201032385/).

Tightening the expectations for Title IX pleased most women and advocates, but was criticized by the College Sports Council. The Council views Title IX as a "gender quota" law and claims that its "current implementation has led to an unnecessary reduction in men's sports" (http://www.mndaily. com/2010/04/25/obama-administration-tightens-title-ix). An article in *Ms. Magazine* counters that it isn't the fault of Title IX when a man's sport is cut to comply with equity requirements. The school is usually "prioritizing big budget sports like football and basketball over 'small' sports like wrestling." According to the article, women's sports have an ongoing struggle for equity under the umbrella of Title IX (http://msmagazine.com/blog/ blog/2010/06/23/title-ix-turns-38-and-its-still-under-attack/).

In looking for balance and parity among the genders, women arguably have made progress since the vote was won. Title IX made other guarantees for women, although as mentioned its status continues to be challenged. We measure status in many ways and economics plays a major role. Do women have the same educational and employment opportunities? Are they paid for their efforts at the same rate as men? Is there as much attention paid to women's health care issues as to those related to men? Does gender make a difference in family standing? Are family responsibilities being shared more equally between spouses/partners?

Economic Issues Impacting Women

Many of us are familiar with the term "glass ceiling," which the U.S. Department of Labor defined in its 1991 "Report on the Glass Ceiling Initiative" as "those artificial barriers based on attitudinal or organizational bias that prevent qualified individuals from advancing upward in their organization into management-level positions" (http://digitalcommons.ilr.cornell. edu/glassceiling/). The commission dealing with this issue existed from 1991–1996 and examined barriers as they apply both to women and to minorities. A variation on the glass ceiling phrase is the "glass elevator" or "glass escalator" which applies to men being promoted more rapidly than women, especially into management positions in female dominated fields such as nursing.

We may be less familiar with the term "Pink Collar Ghetto." If we associate white-collar workers with executive and management positions and blue-collar workers with manual labor, pink collar refers to positions usually associated with women. Those positions are often low-paying non-union jobs providing some sort of service. Beatrix Hoffman, in *Readers Companion to U.S. Women's History,* credits the phrase to the publication of Louise Kapp Howe's *Pink Collar Workers* in 1977. She associates the phrase with occupations such as beautician, waitress, sales clerk, and secretary. Such jobs in the pink-collar ghetto usually provide few benefits with little chance of advancement and may be part-time, seasonal, or temporary according to Howe. In the feminist efforts to address wage discrepancies and equal pay for equal work, they noted that many so-called pink-collar workers had more education than their blue-collar counterparts yet made considerably less money. Comparable worth became the issue. Hoffman claims that the pink-collar ghetto metaphor is being revisited with consideration of the "sticky floor" which effectively traps women in the lowest paid jobs within government bureaucracies and large corporations. According to her, these women are often women of color.

Eden Lin in a 2003 article "Pink-collar ghetto lives on" (*Penn Current* online, February 13, 2003 <http://www.upenn.edu/pennnews/ current/2003/021303/research.html>) says that women are still being paid three-fourths of what men get paid for comparable work, despite the fact that it has been forty years since the passage of equal rights and equal pay legislation. This is based on data provided by the U.S. Census Bureau and analyzed by researchers from three organizations. Their report underscores gender inequality in many forms in the Philadelphia metropolitan area and proposes potential solutions. Their purpose was to increase awareness of women's issues and to "change the way these issues are framed."

Statistics indicate there is an increasing number of single parent families in which women are responsible for the economic soundness of their families. Perpetuating the pay discrepancies for women increases the incidence of poverty, vulnerability to violence, and lack of influence, according to Dana L. Barron, associate director of the Alice Paul Center for Research on Women and Gender. The report cites the significance of segregation of the labor market. It says that women occupy a huge percentage of caregiving jobs, but only a small percentage of women is found among blue-collar jobs that often have union representation. Childcare workers, the people who care for our children, receive pitifully low compensation for their services. What a poor commentary on the value we place on our children, tomorrow's leaders.

Generational Considerations in Protecting Gains Made

We have been discussing the many gains made by courageous women who fought for gender equality. Based on attitudes currently being demonstrated by the upcoming generation of women, it is reasonable to have concerns about maintaining those gains.

Understanding what binds generational cohorts together and what motivates them is helpful in understanding the past and in forecasting the future. Norman Ryder defined these components of demographic analysis in 1965 as "the aggregate of individuals (within some population) who experienced the same event within the same time interval" (*American Sociological Review*, 30, 845). Generational cohorts are groups of people bound together by common experiences which inform their behavior and attitudes. Critics point out that these assessments obviously make generalizations about cohorts which may not apply to all those born within the given time frame. They say it is dangerous to try to retrofit people together and misses out on the rich diversity of individuals.

We acknowledge that there are always exceptions. But information about generational cohorts is used in developing marketing strategies along with predicting future labor needs. For our purposes, it may provide insights about how younger generations of women react to assaults on their rights, as well as urgencies felt by older generations who fought for the rights of all women.

We are probably most aware of the Baby Boomers since advertisements so often reference them. We hear reports about their spending habits, impending retirements, and their plight as the sandwich generation—supporting both children and elderly parents at the same time. Born just after World War II, this generation is compared to the prey in the belly of the python that we watch moving down the snake's body. This huge population paid a lot of taxes and paid into social security. Since the next generation is much smaller, Baby Boomer needs are apt to bankrupt Social Security, according to some economists and analysts. They are also a huge market targeted by industries across the board.

Baby Boomers lived through the assassinations of JFK, RFK, and Martin Luther King, political turmoil, the Vietnam War, the first walk on the moon, the civil rights and women's movements, and the experimental use of "recreational drugs." They are characterized by their free spirit, individualistic approaches, and propensity for social cause. As a group they lived through great changes and also helped effect change.

Baby Boomers were followed by Generation X, born between 1965 and 1976. Gen Xers experienced the Challenger explosion, Reaganomics, AIDS, the fall of the Berlin Wall, the increase in single parent families. They seek emotional security, independence, and informality, and they are characterized as entrepreneurial.

Although there is no consensus about the exact dates for the Generation Y cohort, frequently referred to as the millennials, one of the broadest definitions cites 1977–2002 as the parameters. Although they have grown up with the Internet and communication explosion, this group has also experienced two wars in Iraq and the 9/11 attacks. They are described as technically savvy and seeking physical security because of heightened fears; they are patriotic and accept change. These upcoming leaders of tomorrow are more diverse and better educated than previous generation cohorts. They are, however, impatient and used to the instant gratification of technology. Diplomacy is not their strength and they tend to be very direct and inquisitive. This group also tends to feel "entitled" to their rights but so far seems unwilling to continue the struggle for them.

A study done on Generation Y women revealed that many of these entrepreneurial spirits do not want to be politically involved, other than expressing their opinions in the voting booth. That could prove problematic if tomorrow's female leaders ignore their eroding human rights.

Focus Groups

Statistical data, such as generational cohort data, give us clues and insights about what people think and what influences their thinking; but I have been curious about what "real women" think. Convening focus groups is one way to get at that spirit. We facilitated a total of six focus groups in May–June 2007. I facilitated three in Connecticut (Hartford, Stamford, Mystic), and one in Rhode Island; attorney Deborah Smith Arthur conducted one in Portland, Oregon; and Kaye Delano, a professional counselor, facilitated one in Amelia, Florida. All sessions employed the same questions during a two-hour time frame. Participants represented a cross section of generational cohorts and economic strata. Among them were legal, health, and social service professionals, working mothers, and retirees. While we can't point to the results as statistically valid, the comments appear to substantiate some of the claims we have been making. Their dialogue was both intriguing and provocative.

Each focus group was asked to respond to three basic areas:

- Reaction to Genesis 1–3

- Perception of positive changes since the 1960s Women's Movement and areas still in need of change

- Project status of women to 2017

Genesis 1–3 Reactions

Reaction to Genesis 1–3 was fairly uniform across the board. Some admitted that this was the first time they actually read Genesis, although they were familiar with the wording, as they had heard it read in church. Most were unaware that there are two versions of the creation of man and woman in Genesis and found it perplexing that seemingly contradictory explanations are intact.

Genesis 1: 27–28: *So God created man in his own image, in the image of God he created him; male and female he created them. And God blessed them, and God said to them, "Be fruitful and multiply, and fill the earth and subdue it; and have dominion over the fish of the sea and over birds of the air and over every living thing that moves upon the earth."*

Genesis 2:18: *Then the Lord God said, "It is not good that the man should be left alone; I will make him a helper fit for him.*

Genesis 2:22: . . . *and the rib which the Lord had taken from the man he made into a woman and brought her to the man.*

Reading Genesis 3, the Fall from the Garden section, elicited emotional responses from many who said they felt emotions of shame, guilt, and inferiority, with God and Man in the dominant roles. "It must make God sad," said one woman, "that people take it literally." Others pointed out that there are women from conservative Christian backgrounds who probably feel differently. They might feel that they are truly to blame. Comments indicated that since literalists dominate current politics this opinion continues to impact women's negative views of themselves. One creative thinker commented that her view of this was that Eve took risks and Adam was not a critical thinker. The lesson is that risk takers may have to suffer the consequences of their actions. That's another spin on Garden of Eden story! Most felt that Adam got let off the hook.

All the focus groups indicated that they had felt the consequences of the negative representation of Eve. The range of reactions included personal experiences with gender biases from girlhood as well as feelings of shame, low self-esteem, and the struggle to know and keep their identities. One group discussed strategies used to cope with "outer expectations and restrictions" and the need to compromise themselves to be "acceptable." Still others commented on the implications that sexuality was portrayed as bad and that women were destined to suffer and to be subservient to males.

It is unclear whether or not they still hold those views on sexuality in the twenty-first century; but if so, are such beliefs the result of a reinvigorated Conservative Fundamentalist message? Or is it fear on the part of some women to take responsibility for their own sexuality, preferring to relinquish the "power" to their male partners? Supposedly, the sexual double standard has been dismantled and it is more socially acceptable for women to find pleasure in sexual activities. It is noteworthy, however, that more attention is currently being paid to erectile dysfunction and premature ejaculation than to female frigidity. Are some women fearful of emasculating their men as roles continue to change and become more balanced? Do they subconsciously (or consciously) feel they don't deserve to be happy in their own skin as sisters of Eve? There is much room for further research!

One of the goals of this book is to increase awareness about why women are still held in low esteem by patriarchal organizations and others, and this exercise helped accomplish that goal. The groups concluded that women can even undermine themselves if they believe the sentiment of unworthiness, whether conscious or subconscious.

Perception of Changes since the 1960s Women's Movement

Most agreed with some conviction that the status of women has improved since the 1960s. They either had lived through those decades, heard about them, or read about them. A few argued, however, that the Women's Rights Movement "has hurt women by devaluing homemakers and in many cases making it more difficult for women to work and still have most of the responsibility for child care, meal preparation, etc." There was general consensus among the groups that there is greater access to higher education for women and there are many career choices previously unavailable or closed to women. They also felt that women have greater access to team sports which offers the side benefit of working in a team environment so essential in modern businesses. In addition, most recognized that there are visibly many more women involved in government and politics, although the percentage needs to improve since women comprise 50 percent of the population.

Participants believe that many women are better off economically, in some cases earning salaries close to those made by men in the same positions, but that parity has been reached only in very few areas where job skills are critical and in demand. Women balancing careers and family seemed to think that females could move up the corporate ladder and achieve successes until they had children. From that point they are viewed differently since they have increased home responsibilities and will likely dedicate less time to their careers according to corporate management perspectives. They insist that the glass ceiling is difficult to penetrate. (MomsRising.org, a grass roots organization which recently produced a Motherhood Manifesto Documentary, substantiates that viewpoint.) Others point to strides made in female entrepreneurship growth, a definite improvement.

Several groups claim that consumerism has established the need for two-person breadwinning. They say that the demand for material possessions requires more money to manage households. In addition, people are saving for kids' college tuitions and social security "replacement" funds for retirement. Therefore, there is a double burden. There is an expectation to do more, and women must work harder than husbands since they are the major caregivers—even when men share in the parenting responsibilities. Although they call women who make the choice to stay at home noble, many do not have the means to do so. Many poor women, however, must stay home since they cannot afford childcare. Their choices are more limited.

According to some legal experts on the panels, there is greater legal parity, at least in Connecticut, where there are equal rights in marriage and divorce along with better banking and credit opportunities. They remind us, however, that this aspect varies from state to state. Participants also pointed out that despite improvements, many women remain in dysfunctional, unhappy marriages because they fear they cannot survive and support children on their own. Although there are exceptions, men typically have only themselves to feed, house, and dress. For those divorced men who may have child support responsibilities, far too many become delinquent/deadbeat dads. On the other hand, others countered that many men are now sharing in child custody in a very responsible fashion.

There have been some positive changes and many claimed that more men are sharing in parenting responsibilities; in some cases, stay-at-home dads are primary caregivers when the mom has a good job with benefits. (Perhaps some of the dads are "between jobs.") Expectant couples now say, "We're pregnant," which is indicative of shared responsibility. While these are great trends, according to the groups, women remain the primary caregivers with most of the responsibility and guilt when away from home.

Health care access and coverage remains a major concern among all the groups. They feel that some limited progress has been made among diseases usually associated with women, but much more research and attention is needed. Some felt that too much "R&D" is paid to erectile dysfunction rather than breast cancer. This, they say, is a "pharmaceutically driven" issue with profits as motivation.

Abortions, for those with the means and opportunity to get them, were risky during the early 1960s. They were also illegal! A quick investigation tells us that during the 1800s, criminalization of abortion varied from state to state and by 1910 all but one state made abortion illegal unless absolutely necessary to save a woman's life, as determined by a doctor. Although one-third of the states either liberalized or repealed the criminal abortion laws between 1967 and 1973, it wasn't until the Roe v. Wade Supreme Court decision in 1973 that all women were given the right to have an abortion. Roe v. Wade provided all women the right to legally choose an abortion but in recent years it has come under assault by conservative powers. During the past decade, many states have passed laws severely hampering the impact of Roe v. Wade by imposing restrictions on abortions. Some focus group partici-pants commented, however, that availability of the birth control pill and other contraceptive devices helps alleviate the need for abortions and provide other choices for women, but risk potential health complications and side-effects.

Project Status of Women to 2017

Generally speaking all groups agreed that women are currently better off than in the years prior to the 1970s. There are some projections into the future which are both positive and negative. We will include their forecasts and concerns in the next chapter when we evaluate current gender equality and how it portends for the future.

We have witnessed many changes during the last fifty years. Women have made progress towards equality, occasionally taking three steps forward and two steps back, as the expression goes. In the next chapter we take on the giants and examine where the stumbling blocks exist and why. What is the current status of women in government, organized religion, industry, and big business? Patriarchies still seem to flourish with women in secondary and helper roles. Some women who achieve power appear to undermine rather than help their sisters. Some even seem to sabotage themselves! What can we applaud and what should we fear? What can we do to help bring about balance and gender equality? Stay tuned.

6

Report Card and Prognosis
for the Future

"The history of all time, and of today especially, teaches that . . . women will be forgotten if they forget to think about themselves."

—Louise Otto Peters, 1849

In this chapter we evaluate the actual status of females in the United States, determine stumbling blocks to gender equality and balance, and suggest possible actions and strategies to hasten their achievement. As promised, we scrutinize the giants—patriarchies that seem to flourish with women in secondary and support/helper roles. We also call attention to women themselves—the sometimes destructiveness of women undermining women, as well as those who sabotage themselves.

Let's begin with the obvious question: "What is the current status of women and what grades should we assign?" Progress has been made since the Women's Liberation Movement of the 1960s and '70s, but how can we actually evaluate the current standing of women in the home, at work, and in society in general? There are accusations of backsliding during the last decade; can those setbacks be mitigated or changed? We can report current information with some accuracy and evaluate it.

Let's also pose two questions: How would we *like* the future of American women to look in five to ten years and, more significantly, Is it possible?

Federal Watchdogs/Advocates for the Status of Women

Let's first establish the lay of the land and objectively determine the current status of women, with an eye to anticipate future changes for better or worse. Hoping to consult national agencies representing and advocating for women's issues for help on this, I looked for ones devoted to the status of women. What current federal agencies, commission, or committees, I wondered, are carrying forward the work begun with the Commission on the Status of Women established by President Kennedy in 1961? I discovered that there is no longer any official federal agency responsible for monitoring the progress and rights of women. Many had hoped that this would change with the election of Barack Obama, but women's groups were disappointed when President Obama created an interagency task force rather than a Cabinet level office or Presidential Commission.

As mentioned earlier, each state does have a Commission on the Status of Women; but structures, functions, and missions vary. There also is an *international* agency that monitors women's rights, the Convention on the Elimination of All Forms of Discrimination against Women (CDEAW). It was organized under the auspices of the United Nations in 1946, originally as a subcommission of the Commission on Human Rights. But while the welfare of all women is a concern to us, our focus in this chapter is on the status of women in the United States.

There are numerous private and independent groups and foundations in the United States whose mission is dedicated to the status of women—which makes the disconnect at the national (federal) level seem peculiar. In a recent interview, Connecticut Congresswoman Rosa DeLauro indicated, however, that while official federal agencies dealing specifically with the status of women are not obvious, the organizational structure does have components that include attention to women's issues. She points to the following areas which I subsequently investigated.

- **Department of Labor**

  A Women's Bureau was created in the 1920s under the Department of Labor "to represent the employment needs of America's working women." It "carries out its mission through demonstration projects and partnerships with firms, universities, and other organizations in order to improve working conditions for women." But a recent program assessment revealed by ExpectMore.gov is critical of the Bureau, claiming that "results were not demonstrated" and outlining corrective actions. (The program assessment is at www.whitehouse.gov/omb/expectmore/summary/10003906.2005.html).

- **Department of Health Services**

  Although it is not displayed on the organizational chart, there is an Office on Women's Health (OWH) under the U.S. Department of Health and Human Services (DHHS). Established in 1991, the Office aims to ensure that "all women and girls are healthier and have a better sense of well being." The Office's mission is to "provide leadership to promote health equity for women and girls through sex/gender-specific approaches." To accomplish this, the Office develops innovative programs, by "educating health professionals, and motivating behavior change in consumers through dissemination of health information."

  The National Institutes of Health (NIH), is also under the jurisdiction of the DHHS and is the "Nation's Research Agency." Although women and minorities were not included in earlier studies, that practice has apparently changed.

- **US Food and Drug Administration (FDA)**

  The U.S. Food and Drug Administration also oversees an Office of Women's Health. There was an attempt to phase out the OWH by the FDA but Congress blocked that effort, according to Congresswoman Delauro.

- **Department of Veterans Affairs**

  Women's Veterans Issues addresses the needs of female veterans, including military sexual trauma, special monthly compensation and health care for women veterans.

- **Equal Employment Opportunity Commission**

  The EEOC is an independent agency of the U.S. government, created by Title VII of the Civil Rights Act of 1964. Its mission and scope have been modified by laws, amendments, and executive orders, but the Commission enforces six basic laws:

- Title VII of the Civil Rights Act
- Equal Pay Act of 1963
- Age Discrimination in Employment Act of 1967
- Rehabilitation Act of 1973
- Titles I and V of the Americans with Disabilities Act of 1990, and
- Civil Rights Act of 1991. The laws informing EEOC actions, however, are subject to interpretation by the federal court system and the Supreme Court.

• **Department of Education**

The Office for Civil Rights, under the auspices of the U.S. Department of Education, is responsible for gender equity in education issues as well as sexual harassment and complaints.

• **Bi-Partisan Women's Caucus**

Originally called the Congresswomen's Caucus in 1977, the name was changed to the Congressional Caucus for Women's Issues when men were invited to join in 1981. The caucus convenes to promote issues they consider important for all women. It also focuses on international women's issues and other areas where agreement is possible. (That de facto excludes discussion of areas relating to abortion.) The Senate does not have a similar caucus but female senators meet informally with some regularity. Despite the inclusion of women's issues in those departments, there remains no cabinet level or department level appointee, and no ombudsman overseeing the rights of women.

Assessment

Now that we've set the stage a bit with background information, let's structure our assessment. In light of the concerns and forecasts of the focus groups mentioned in chapter five, we find their concerns seemed to fall into six general categories, some of which overlap:
- Home, Church, and Society
- Education
- Health and Health Care

- Workplace Discrepancies and Inequities
- Politics, Government, and Law
- Media Representation of Women

Home, Church, Society

In the past ten years, women have been adding more and more to their already long list of responsibilities. Although shared parenting in some families has lessened the burden, most married women have to work at least part-time to help the family afford the mortgage and accoutrements of our accumulation-driven society. Economic impacts at this writing put further pressures on families to increase their incomes in a struggling economy. In addition, childcare needs are more and more challenging as the competence of providers is called into question. Many offspring are involved in after-school sports and events requiring Mom's support and taxi service. Women might also be responsible for care and/or supervision of aging parents. Single moms and poor women have additional concerns and issues.

Sadly, domestic abuse continues to plague our society as well: At the turn of this century, estimates on incidents of violence against a current or former spouse, boyfriend, or girlfriend ranged from 960,000 per year to three million women being physically abused each year by a husband or boyfriend. This report is according to an article entitled "Domestic Violence is a Serious, Widespread Social Problem in America: The Facts," which also provides many other disturbing facts about domestic abuse (library.adoption. com/articles/domestic-violence-is-a-serious-widespread-social-problem-in-America-the-facts.html).

Violence against Women and Domestic Abuse

Domestic violence primarily impacts women. Two government agencies, the Department of Health and Human Services and the U.S. Department of Justice, have been addressing these issues. The DOJ monitors them through its Office on Violence Against Women (OVW); the Department of Health and Human Services (DHHS) provides information regarding the topic on womenshealth.gov.

Women have been victims of verbal, physical, and sexual abuse over the centuries. Why do so many continue to remain in their abusive relationships? Focus groups conducted by the OVW speculate that "victims may struggle with an extremely complex emotional, psychological, even monetary calculus before finally deciding to leave their abusers" ("Awareness and Attitudes About Domestic Violence," p. 2 <http://www.ovw.usdoj.gov/docs/polling_summary.pdf>). They go onto say, "Shame, low self-esteem, and fear of repercussions from the perpetrator as well as a financial inability to leave can combine to create a figurative prison that grips women." One-third of the participants, however, place some blame on the victim for not leaving the abusive situation.

On January 5, 2006, the Violence Against Women Act was reauthorized, having been first passed in 1994. Stalking and dating violence had been added to the list of crimes in 2000, but the new law added additional programs and services including:

- violence prevention programs
- new protections for victims who are evicted from their apartments because they are victims of domestic violence and/or stalking
- funding for rape crisis centers
- programs to meet the needs of women of different races or ethnicities
- more programs and services for victims with disabilities
- services for children and teens.

The Department of Health and Human Services provided the above information and reported a 49 percent drop in the number of nonfatal, violent acts committed by intimate partners between 1993 and 2001. Although that is certainly good news, some are skeptical. The National Coalition Against Domestic Violence, for example, which represents the concerns of battered women and their families, believes that "violence against women and children results from the use of force or threat to achieve and maintain control over others in intimate relationships, and from societal abuse of power and domination in the forms of sexism, racism, homophobia, classism, anti-Semitism, able-bodyism, ageism and other oppressions" (http://www.ncadv.org/aboutus.php). NCADV has a multifaceted approach working for "major societal changes necessary to eliminate both personal and societal violence against all women and children."

It is reassuring to know there are both public and private agencies working on such a daunting problem as domestic abuse and violence; but much more needs to be done to help women help themselves with economic assistance, psychological counseling, and better protection from their abusers. Until such women feel better about their self-worth and potential abusers are stopped in their tracks, the problem will persist.

Religious empowerment and marginalization

Churches play a major role in the structure of American society, and the last several decades have seen a religious resurgence in certain parts of the country. Organized religion has played significant roles in our politics, influencing how people vote and what postures they take on social issues. Although there are exceptions to the rule, many organized religions are patriarchal in nature and unfortunately do not consider women to be equal partners to men. Unfortunately that posture influences the permissibility of women's ordination within the given religious tradition. There are exceptions to that exclusionary rule, some more surprising than others.

Included among the current exceptions are some of the Jewish denominations. A Rabbinical Assembly admitted females into Conservative Judaism in 1985, and Reform Judaism and Reconstructionists also approved females as Rabbinical candidates. Although Orthodox Jews employ female "congregational interns," the interns are not allowed to lead worship services but are permitted to preach, teach, and consult on Jewish law.

Society of Friends, known as Quakers, seems to be one of the earliest Christian denominations to ordain women. They base their policy on John 20:17 which indicates that there is an element of God's spirit in every person so every person has an inherent and equal value, regardless of gender. The Unitarian/Universalist Church was also an early exception and became the first large denomination to have a majority of female ministers. The Salvation Army has always ordained both men and women since their inception around 1865. In 1956, Methodist Protestants accorded women full clergy rights and conference membership. Other Protestant denominations, including some Presbyterians, some Baptists, Evangelical Lutherans and Episcopalians also approve female ordination. It is estimated that approximately half of all Protestant denominations ordain women as ministers. Only a handful, however, allow women to become bishops (http://www.religioustolerance. org/femclrg13.htm). Eastern religions such as Buddhism, which allows full ordination of Buddhist nuns, and Hinduism, Shinto, and Taoism appear to view women more equally by ordaining both men and women.

As a rule, conservative faith-based groups deny ordination for women because of their convictions that women have specific roles within the church and family that preclude their participation as top church leaders. Positions of authority and power are reserved for men. Included in this category are the Roman Catholic Church, Eastern Orthodox churches, some provinces of the Anglican Communion, The Church of Jesus Christ of Latter-Day Saints (Mormon), and additional fundamentalist and evangelical Protestant denominations. It is worth noting that there are two denominations that ordained women at one time but have stopped. The Presbyterian Church of Australia in 1991 and the Southern Baptist Convention in the U.S. in 2000 were both involved in situations in which fundamentalists took over a formerly more moderate denomination and rescinded women's rights to ordination (http://www.religioustolerance.org/femclrg13.htm)

The marginalization of women by organized religion is well illustrated by a story featured in *Good Morning America* on February 18, 2008, about a female referee who was not allowed to participate in that capacity at St. Mary's Academy in Topeka, Kansas. Michelle Campbell was not allowed to referee a boy's basketball game there because, according Principal Father Vincent Griego, "Placing women in positions of authority over men is contrary to our beliefs."

Supposedly this church subscribes to "older Roman Catholic laws," but what is the message? The television commentator noted that there are female teachers who teach boys and asked if that was an exception. Father Griego did not respond to requests for interviews or clarifications. Rick Dean reported in

The Capital-Journal, a Topeka newspaper, that Michelle's referee partner, Darin Putthoff, was shocked and said he would leave also if she had to leave. The Associated Press explains that St. Mary's is owned and operated by the Society of St. Pius X, "a priestly society founded by Archbishop Marcel Lefebvre that opposes changes made by the Roman Catholic Church during the 1960s."

I recently discovered an organization called the Women's Justice Coalition (WJC). It's actually one of a conglomeration of organizations coordinated by *Catholics Speak Out*, a program of the Quixote Center. The people involved with the Center describe themselves (http://quixote.org/about) as a "band of impossible dreamers" who came together in 1976 as a multi-issue, grassroots social organization rooted in Catholic justice tradition but independent from church and government structures. They subscribe to the tenet that "an educated and engaged citizenry is essential to making social change." Their name derives from their admiration of the "satiric idealism and gentle madness of Cervantes' dauntless Don Quixote." Their mission is to work on "issues of justice with people who have few other resources," employing humor in their process. The Quixote Center attracts people of faith and conscience from a diverse population dedicated to peace and justice and claims to include seventy thousand people among their friends, associates, and donors. The Women's Justice Coalition is one of the many groups they support.

The Women's Justice Coalition aspires to bring about reform and renewal within the Roman Catholic Church. Their annual action project spotlights women's equality while building a grassroots movement of those supporting "equality and justice for women." Their credo (http://cso.quixote.org/node/79) includes the following affirmations:

The time has come

- To affirm the equal rights of women and men in the church

- To share decision-making with women and men equally

- For our liturgical ministries to reflect the equality we proclaim

- For inclusive language, the language of hospitality, to be the norm for our preaching, our liturgy, and church documents

- To acknowledge that the Holy Spirit calls women, as well as men, to ordained ministry

The Coalition's rationale for the equality call is based on the Church's baptismal formula and the language of the Second Vatican Council in 1965. First, according to Galatians 3:27–28 regarding baptism they quote: "Each one of you is a child of God because of your faith in Christ Jesus. All of you who have been baptized into Christ have clothed yourselves in Christ. In Christ, there is no Jew or Greek, slave or citizen, male or female. All are one in Jesus Christ." The second part of their rationale refers to the Second Vatican Council decree which states, "With respect to the fundamental rights of the person, every type of discrimination, whether social or cultural, whether based on sex, race, color, social condition, language or religion, is to be overcome and eradicated as contrary to God's intent" (*Pastoral Constitution on the Church in the Modern World*: 29 December, 1965, Part I, Chapter II, 29).

The group lauds progress made for women in other religious institutions and civil societies, but bemoans evidence that Roman Catholic leaders "have failed to practice what they preach."

According to the WJC, 97 percent of Catholics of all generations support participation of lay people in parish governance, 62 percent of all U.S. Catholics are supportive of women priests, and 81 percent of all Catholics support ordination of women to the deaconate.

The (WJC) Report Card Project

This project taken up by the Coalition analyzes for the first time the status of women in the Church and indicates that there are wide disparities in the roles of men and women. Professor Susan Farrell, a lead analyst in this report, quotes Pope Benedict XVI's statement that it is "theologically and anthropologically important for women to be at the center of Christianity." Professor Farrell assigns an F to the dioceses regarding representation of women in religious education and a D in hiring women for upper level jobs. (Originally posted online at the WJC Web site, copies of the report are now available through www.futurechurch.org.)

The Coalition's surveys indicate the status of women in seminaries, on diocesan councils, and in diocesan employment scenarios and report some good news and some bad news. Women have made progress in visibility as lectors at cathedral liturgies, but girls are not often used as altar servers when bishops preside over masses. Another project leader, Professor Regina Bannan, underscores the need for Bishops to provide complete information to seminarians and lay church members about the roles women played in the early church. According to Bannan, "The failure to learn our own history lies at the heart of many of today's disagreements" (http://blog.cbeinternational. org/2007/05/).

I agree with Bannan's assessment at several levels since we speculate that many, perhaps most, Roman Catholics have no idea about the role women have played since the early days of Christianity. As far as people are concerned, men played the leadership roles in the formation and expansion of Christianity and women played support roles. As a result of new information revealed within the last several decades, we now know for certain that women did play major leadership roles. Furthermore, the Church has always cited Genesis 1–3 to justify the marginalization of women and loyal parishioners bought into it. When new information was discovered and revealed, the revisions rarely trickled down to the grass roots. After all, parity of women in the Church would not be in the perceived best interests of some.

Women's Justice Coalition Conclusions and Recommendations

The WJC project concludes that solid progress has been made in the U.S. Roman Catholic Church since Vatican II, citing the following improvements:

- Women and girls perform liturgical functions formerly reserved for men and boys.

- Against Vatican urging, most bishops in the surveyed dioceses include women along with men in the foot-washing ceremony, symbolic of Jesus' teaching that leaders must be servants to the people they serve and the underlying principle of equal treatment of followers, "regardless of social or ecclesial rank."

- Generally speaking, there are nearly equal numbers of men and women serving as lectors and Eucharist ministers in Cathedral liturgies; when the bishops are not there, girls often are allowed to serve on the altar.

- Most bishops acknowledge that some economic assistance is appropriate for men and women serving in the lay ministry.

The Report Card Project researchers indicate that although gains have been made, improvement is needed. Specifically, seminarians are not provided with an understanding and appreciation of the role and scope of women's contributions to Christianity, or of the Church's misogynistic teachings. In addition, very few women are employed among seminary faculty, which helps to perpetuate the marginalization of women.

Recommendations for Change

Based on their survey of twenty-three U.S. dioceses and archdioceses, the WJC project concludes that there is significant foot-dragging by bishops when it comes to follow-through on key Church teachings about women. They make the following recommendations:

1. *End faculty discrimination and teach seminarians about the history of women in Christianity.*

Bishops are asked to end discrimination against female faculty and to require that curricula for seminarians include developments in Church history and biblical interpretation as well as incorporation of courses on "historical contributions of women and the teachings that legitimized discrimination against women."

The Coalition feels that such curricula are necessary as women were "held to be morally, mentally, and physically inferior to men by many generations of Catholics." They add that all Catholics "need a deeper understanding of how the Church's theology of the reality of sin in human life has changed, together with the theological basis for restricting Holy Orders to men only." That is to say, the basis for refusing to allow women into the priesthood is flawed and needs reform.

2. *Incorporate biblical and historic roles of women into Catholic education.*

Children, adolescents, and adults should learn about women's roles in the Church's history in age-appropriate increments. They need to understand the nature of theological development as well as Jesus' respect for women and his inclusive practices.

The Coalition claims that Church leaders may give lip service to the equality, but their actions do not demonstrate their commitment to equality. Catholics should be taught about the nature of women with examples of competent and inspiring women leaders and the development of religious orders.

3. *Representation of women on advisory boards.*

Bishops are asked to promote integrating women into their advisory boards and encouraged to establish pastoral advisory boards if they do not already have them. They are also called upon to develop financial advisory councils and Catholic Charities boards, seeking a variety of representatives from diverse ethnic, socioeconomic, and educational backgrounds. This effort will potentially help the Church "rediscover its Gospel roots and reclaim its soul in service to the poor and disadvantaged."

4. *Representation of women in top administrative positions.*

Although the bishops have made great progress in including women in their upper administration (and have done better than secular industry) the status of women in the Vatican bureaucracy needs much improvement.

5. *Just employee and conflict resolution practices.*

The Coalition cites the National Association of Church Personnel Administrators and the Emerging Models for Parish Leadership Project of the Lilly Endowment as a source for developing better relationships between bishops, the laity, and their employees. Those groups are collaborating with six Catholic organizations in the development of model resources for pastoral leaders. Poor hiring and conflict resolution practices are viewed as major reasons for the poor relationships.

6. *Future studies about justice for women in the Church.*

The Coalition asks the Catholic academics to examine the Church's progress towards equality for women, noting movement away from its "historic ambivalence and even hostility toward women."

The study conducted by the Women's Justice Coalition is certainly enlightening and supports some of the claims that many have been making. Allowing priests to marry and to choose or not choose celibacy remain hot issues within the American Roman Catholic Church. Permitting women to become priests, however, seems unlikely under the current papacy.

Pope Benedict XVI has made some changes and played a role in eliminating the concept of Limbo. His chief astronomer even declared recently, "Believing that the universe may contain alien life does not contradict a faith in God." Those are positive changes. The Pope continues to cling to the traditional view, however, that Jesus chose only men as his apostles and therefore never intended women to be priests. In fact the Vatican announced a warning in May 2008 that women participating in "so-called ordinations" will be excommunicated (http://msnbc.msn.com/id/24894993). The same article quotes Monsignor Angelo Amato of the Doctrine of the Faith as saying, "The Church does not feel authorized to change the will of its founder Jesus Christ." The Vatican newspaper published the decree, calling women's ordination a "crime" in the headline. It reported that the congregation said it acted to "preserve the nature and validity of the sacrament" of ordination.

According to Victor Simpson, a writer for the Associated Press, the archbishop of St. Louis excommunicated three women in 2008 for participating in an ordination. The ordination was part of the Roman Catholic Womenpriests movement (which began in 2002); two of the women were American and one was South African African (http://www.newsvine.com/_news/2008/05/30/1523799-vatican-excommunication-for-female-priests). Simpson also quotes Vittorio Bellavite, associated with the international reform group *We Are Church*, who says, "We didn't expect anything different now, but in 20 to 30 years they will be expressing their regrets when they will need more priests." It appears that the Church hierarchy considers women to be equal to men in many aspects, but not equal enough.

U.S. women in religious orders were the targets of an investigation initiated by the Vatican in 2009. This disturbing development put in place an examination of the conduct of U.S. nuns through "visitations of religious orders" and an "umbrella organization," the Leadership Conference of Women Religious. LCWR has approximately 1500 members representing

68,000 (95 percent) of all U.S. women in religious orders. Several nuns told the *New York Times* that they feared the Church was attempting to return to old, pre-Vatican II traditions such as wearing habits, living in convents, and working in Church institutions.

From other comments I've heard and read about, they are not alone in their concerns. Cardinal William Levada, for example, head of the Congregation for the Doctrine of the Faith, charges that LCWR has not complied with Church teaching on homosexuality, the men-only priesthood, and considering the Catholic Church as the only means of salvation. The LCWR must respond to those complaints. Furthermore, according to Thomas C. Fox of the *National Catholic Reporter* (July 6, 2010 <http://ncronline.org/news/women-religious/vatican-officials-us-women-religious-meet>), Cardinal Franc Rodé, prefect of the Congregation for Institutes of Consecrated Life and Societies of Apostolic Life, has begun his own investigation to assess the "quality of life" among U.S. Women religious communities and to investigate the cause of decline in their numbers. Rodé has appointed Mother Clare Millea, superior general of the Apostles of the Sacred Heart of Jesus, as the "apostolic visitator."

We will be watching for the results of the investigations. Will the Church actually retreat further back into the old ways supported by some ultra-conservative viewpoints? It is unfortunate that as much emphasis and energy hasn't been placed on the child abuse scandal permeating the Church.

We are making some progress in the Home, Church, and Society category, but much remains to be done. Unfortunately, we sometimes take three steps forward and two steps back. We'll take a look at changes we'd like to see and their chances for success later in this chapter.

Education

It is quite clear from statistical data that women have made significant progress in accessing and attending college and graduate schools. In fact, a January 26, 2010 article in *USA Today* (http://www.usatoday.com/news/education/2010-01-26-genderequity26_ST_N.htm) reports that the "gender gap" on campus for enrollment and bachelor's degrees has remained stable at around 57 percent of women since 2000. Women continue to take advantage of higher education opportunities, thanks in part to the women's movement and Title IX.

Ironically, there is great consternation among some who fear that society is in trouble if men fail to attend college in larger numbers. They claim that colleges tend to appeal more to women's learning styles and interests. Tamar Lewin stated in a July 9, 2006 *New York Times* article, "At Colleges, Women are Leaving Men in the Dust," that according to Department of Education statistics, men are less likely than women to complete their bachelor's degrees and tend to get lower grades. The article goes on to say, however, that men are *not* in "a downward spiral" as they are going to college in increasing numbers and are more likely to graduate than they were twenty years ago.

The higher percentage of women in college has had a positive impact on societal values in the student populations. Lewin also cites experts who claim that girls are more interested in the status of their GPA and how they look on paper. Yet, despite their gains in academic prowess, women still lag behind men in wages for equal work performed. We discuss the gender wage gap and the battle for equal pay for equal jobs performed later in this chapter.

Why So Few?, published in 2010 by AAUW, examines the small percentage of women in what they call STEM (Science, Technology, Engineering and Math) areas. According to the report, there have been controversial assessments about potential innate differences between men and women relative to scientific or mathematical ability. The study found that people tend to associate men with science and technology and women with humanities and arts areas. This "implicit bias" predisposes genders to particular fields and "people often hold negative opinions of women in 'masculine' positions, like scientists or engineers" (p. xvi). The research also indicates that women must clearly excel to be considered competent in a "masculine" job, yet when she proves herself to be competent, she is less apt to be considered "likeable." It is a real conundrum. The study underscores that the classical formula has long been held that men naturally excel in mathematics demanding disciplines and women naturally excel in fields requiring language skills. Much of this, they say, is because of cultural attitudes and demonstrates the need for learning environments to cultivate abilities and interests without bias or stereotype (p. xiv). Lisa Maatz at AAUW claims that getting more American women involved in STEM fields isn't just an issue of equality, it's also an issue of keeping America competitive in technology and innovation. She goes on to say, "Having an adequately prepared STEM workforce is about homeland security and national defense and high-tech jobs that would be here on American soil." Ms. Maatz feels that we currently have an "incredibly leaky" pipeline (http://www.newsweek.com/2010/06/29/steming-the-tide.html).

Women have a purpose in college—to get ahead, become self-sufficient, and succeed as independent people. This is a far cry from the days when many women reportedly went to universities to meet their future husbands. In the movie *Mona Lisa Smile*, for example, the art history professor played by Julia Roberts was disillusioned to observe that many of her brightest students at Wellesley were leaving to marry eligible Ivy League bachelors—relinquishing claim to their own potential careers. They were intelligent women of privilege who had access to higher education because of family money and power but were more committed to finding a love match than completing an education. (Parenthetically, I remember elder aunts telling me that if I didn't meet a potential husband in college, I would be an "old maid." For the record, I did *not* meet that special person in college, but I ultimately did get married . . . and divorced.)

Increasing attendance of women in college is indeed an improvement, but the focus groups we conducted were also concerned about curricular shortcomings in K–12. Many of their participants felt that women's issues and history need to be taught as a regular part of all curricula to help students understand the struggle for equality during the Women's Movement. It's no wonder that Generation Y females feel entitled, without comprehending how their foremothers fought so hard for "rights" they take so much for granted.

Related to educational concerns among the focus groups was the lack of engagement of Generation Y women. As stated earlier, that generation cohort is reputed to be apathetic, feeling entitled and reluctant to become politically involved other than by expressing their satisfaction at the polling booth, or not. Thanks to Connecticut's AAUW president, Carol Virostek, I met two inspirational and energized young women who are exceptions to the cohort characterization.

As fourteen-year-old Girl Scouts from Ridgefield, Connecticut, Amrita

Sankar and Allison Dziuba decided to research the status of women as part of a silver medal project. Little did they know how far their research would reach and the number of lives they would touch!

With some assistance from AAUW, the best friends developed curricula for girls and women to examine historical representations of women, their current status, and present challenges. In *From Apathy to Activism: Engaging the Younger Generation in the Equity Mission* they contend that modern girls do not know about priority issues for women. Their statement further contends: "What appears to be apathy among most K-12 girls is really a lack of awareness to gender issues in women's history, status, activism, or legislation." They encourage women and young female leaders to connect with this Y generation to help the advancement of equity.

Amrita and Allison view intergenerational dialogue as a vehicle for increasing awareness of gender "inequity" with the hope of inspiring young women to take action. This educational approach "emphasizes ways activists can use their resources and leadership skills to accomplish AAUW issue priorities." The program concept they initiated and presented at the 2007 AAUW convention, holds real promise for replication or adaptation across the country: Education is the key to change.

Although there has been no clear adaptation of their program to date, it is appropriate to note that there are signs on the Internet that units emphasizing women's contributions to world history are being used in home schooling (see, for example, www.womeninworldhistory.com/current.html#anchor-Women's-49575). And, if increasing awareness is a key to underscoring female contributions to the world and society, Women's History Month helps focus on those contributions. In addition, there are more than eight hundred Women's Studies programs worldwide which should surely capture the enthusiasm for women's issues and contributions. Hopefully, all of those activities will begin to filter down to the youngsters in elementary school while they are in their formative years.

In their presentation, the young women discuss the jump-start Title IX provides for women, yet point out the need for vigilance as the regulation is currently under assault. Let's use that as a segway to examine Title IX, its academic relevance and status, for ourselves.

Title IX

Title IX of the Education Amendments of 1972 (also known as the Patsy T. Mink Equal Opportunity in Education Act), became law in June, 1972. It simply states, "No person shall, on the basis of sex, be excluded from participation in, be denied the benefits of, or be subjected to discrimination under any education program or activity receiving Federal financial assistance." Although most people associate this law with high school and collegiate athletic opportunities, the original law did not specify athletics as such. The controversy seemed to arise after a three-prong test of compliance was instituted in 1979 under Jimmy Carter's administration. The U.S. Department of Health, Education, and Welfare based the test on the following.

Prong one: Providing athletic opportunities that are substantially proportionate to the student enrollment, OR

Prong two: Demonstrate a continual expansion of athletic opportunities for the underrepresented sex, OR

Prong three: Full and effective accommodation of the interest and ability of the underrepresented sex.

According to the process, those receiving federal funds must demonstrate compliance with Title IX by meeting *any one* of the three prongs. Although Title IX is not considered to be a quota system but rather an attempt at parity, its critics claim that athletic opportunities are taken away from male students and given to female students instead of accomplishing the original intent of the law—which is preventing academic discrimination. Proponents counter that the three-prong test promotes broader sports participation for women who were not allowed to participate before. They also claim that male collegiate sport participation actually has increased since the initiation of Title IX and that "non-revenue" sports were on the way out prior to Title IX. Furthermore, scholarship allocations must represent the ratio of female and male athletes so that compliance ensures fairness for both genders.

Despite Title IX's thirty-five years of resounding success in fighting sex discrimination, however, the Department of Education under the Bush administration pulled back on its enforcement at the high school level. Schools were allowed to merely send emails to determine female interest in specific sports. Failure to respond was assumed to be disinterest and the schools were considered to be in compliance. Furthermore, beginning in 2005, high school level institutions were not required to report data regarding athletic opportunity, participation, and funding. In response to that relaxation of enforcement, The High School Athletics Accountability Act of 2007 was introduced, intending to require that such information be provided. HR 901, seeking to amend the Elementary and Secondary Act of 1965, was referred to the House Sub-committee on Early Childhood, Elementary, and Secondary Education on June 5, 2007.

A Title IX red flag was raised when the Department of Education issued a "Notification of Intent to Regulate" in 2002 and in 2004 proposed modifications to regulations that make it easier for single-sex schools and classes to discriminate than to protect against sex discrimination. Many schools were outraged and opposed to the proposed legislation. In April 2004 the National Coalition for Women and Girls in Education sent a protest letter to Assistant Secretary of Education Marcus.

This powerful coalition of more than fifty organizations had a mission to improve educational opportunities for women and girls. They argued that Title IX is imperative for protecting the rights of all students and that the Department's proposals would severely weaken the effectiveness of the existing standards and deteriorate "the basic protections against sex discrimination in education." According to their thinking, "the proposed regulations allow school districts to exclude girls or boys from classrooms or schools based on harmful sex stereotypes . . ."

The Coalition further questioned the authority of the Department of Education to revise Title IX regulations. Susan Klein in *Title IX and Single Sex Education* says that "all but about 100 of the 5000 public comments objected to these proposed regulations and they have not been issued" (http://feminist. org/education/pdfs/SingleSex.pdf).

Fortunately, the Department of Education under the Obama administration reversed the Bush administration policy in 2010, reinstating Title IX protections to women and girls, thanks in part to the efforts of National Women's Law Center, National Coalition for Women and Girls in Education, and American Association of University Women.

Such challenges remind us to be vigilant about erosion of gains made. It is disturbing to observe an undercurrent of fear that unwittingly or deliberately seeks to undermine efforts made to equalize opportunities for males and females. What is the basis of such fear?

There are some who would have us believe that gains made by girls have been at the expense of boys and cite a "boys' crisis" in education. The AAUW determined that there is no basis for such an assertion. In their 2008 report, "Where the Girls Are: The Facts about Gender Equity in Education" (http://www.aauw.org/learn/research/WhereGirlsAre.cfm), researchers used data from standardized tests such as NAEP, SAT, ACT, etc. The indicators show that although girls have made great strides in many areas, boys also have improved or remained the same in educational achievement. They determined that the "crisis" is more appropriately assigned to African Americans, Hispanic, and low-income children and is not specific to boys.

It is clear that there is an urgent need to make changes in curricula to include women's issues, history, rights, etc., at various levels beginning in grade school. Perhaps learning the truth about the need for equality at an early age might sensitize males and females to respect each other as equals. We have made great strides in the education category; but to continue the journey forward, we must be vigilant about protecting those gains, and resolute in our commitment to continued improvement. It should be no surprise that education is the key to success in so many of the categories we are discussing.

Health and Health Care

Health care issues for women were of paramount concern in all our focus groups, in particular cures for women's diseases and health care access. It appears that the focus group concerns with the status of health and health care for women in the U.S. are warranted, according to a recently released report compiled by the National Women's Law Center (NWLC) and Oregon Health and Science University. "Making the Grade on Women's Health: a National and State Report Card" (http://hrc.nwlc.org/) clearly provides documentation for two major conclusions:

1. "For the bulk of indicators of the status of women's health, the nation as a whole and the individual states are falling further behind in their quest to reach national goals for women's health."

On page 7 of the Women's Health Report Card, NWLC cites a report issued in 2007 by Healthy People 2010 (http://www.healthypeople. gov/), a national health and promotion and disease prevention initiative managed by the U.S. Department of Health and Human Services. According to that report, women's health does not come close to desired goals and is given a general grade of "unsatisfactory." Nationally, only three goals out of twenty-seven benchmarks established in 2007 were considered as having been approached in a "satisfactory" manner. Those include the number of regular mammograms by women over forty, an increase in the number of women receiving colorectal cancer screenings, and women making annual dental visits. The nation's failure to meet twelve out of twenty-seven indicators, however, is up from failing at nine in 2004. The report goes on to say that the implications are even greater than the numbers suggest, as nationwide there are disparities in the quality of women's health as it relates to race, ethnicity, sexual orientation, and disability.

Even worse than the national statistics are the state indicators. According to the NWLC Report Card, all states failed to meet benchmarks in areas critical to women's overall health—including access to health insurance. Shockingly, no state meets the goals established for increasing women's pap smears and reducing obesity—two goals previously met in the 2004 report. Twelve states received overall failing grades for their weak performance, up from seven in 2004. We are moving in the wrong direction!!

2. "States have made more progress in adopting policies to advance women's health than they have in previous report cards, but still have a long way to go."

This is certainly a mixed bag of information. Some states have made progress while others have regressed. Medicaid coverage for smoking cessation improved across the board and twenty states made improvements in minimum wage levels. The report goes on to summarize the status on page 9:

• The nation still receives an overall grade of unsatisfactory.

• No state received an overall grade of satisfactory.

- In addition to the two benchmarks met by the nation in the past—the percentage of women getting mammograms regularly and the number of dental visits—in 2007 the benchmark is also met for the percentage of women age fifty and older who receive screenings for colorectal cancer.

- Though the most improved status indicators among states were stroke and coronary heart disease death rates, the country still receives an overall F grade in these two indicators because so much improvement is still needed.

- All states declined in the obesity status indicator.

- The most improved policies among states were coverage of smoking cessation services in Medicaid and increases in the minimum wage.

- The most declined policies among the states were co-payments on prescription drugs covered by Medicaid and requiring waiting periods for women who need an abortion.

- Only two policy goals were met by all states: Medicaid coverage for breast and cervical cancer treatments and participation in the Food Stamp Nutrition and Education Program (FSNEP).

The authors of the report are critical of the "Affordability Gap in Women's Health Coverage" (http://hrc.nwlc.org/Federal-Policy-Agenda.aspx). According to their research, more than seventeen million women have no health insurance at all, an "alarming increase" from past statistics. Generally speaking, women experience significantly different circumstances than men for a number of reasons, including the likelihood of lower incomes and lower probability of health care coverage through their employers—even though they need to use more health care services. Furthermore, "Women have higher out-of-pocket costs than men as a share of their income." As a result, they tend to avoid needed health care they can't afford. Finally, women tend to have more medical bills and debt challenges than men.

Federal and administration policy changes in the last few years of the Bush administration have negatively influenced the status of women, in particular poor women, and their basic needs. Both Medicare and Medicaid have taken significant hits, weakening the provision of health care programs for women. The Medicare Prescription Drug Improvement and Modernization Act of 2003 complicated the federal program and severely impacted the lowest income beneficiaries, especially women. Suspension of secondary drug coverage through Medicaid left the poorest Medicare beneficiaries with few options for expensive prescriptions, according to NWLC. The gap, referred to as a "donut hole," caps the benefits for Part D beneficiaries meeting the initial coverage limit and requires that they pay the full costs for any drugs beyond the cap. One then would have to reach the "catastrophic coverage" ceiling in order to receive any more help. If Medicaid were restructured as the Bush administration recommended, it would have been configured as a block grant with allocations to each state to determine eligibility. In that format, funds would be limited and therefore some deserving people would be denied services. Since more women than men have benefited from this program, they would have been disproportionately affected. After the NWLC report was published, a new Obama administration was determined to complete health reform legislation that was ultimately passed by the House in March, 2010. The Medicare Part D language purports to close the so-called donut hole for seniors and low-income beneficiaries as it is phased in over the next ten years (http://docs.house.gov/energycommerce/Summary.pdf).

The NWLC report also commented on the implications of the Bush tax cuts (for the wealthy, some say), explaining that the cuts made fewer dollars available for women's health needs to those who need it the most. Furthermore, according to them, the timing couldn't be worse for such cuts, with baby boomers retiring in droves and having to meet the resulting greater costs with less income.

Reproductive Rights

Reproductive rights for women is both a social issue and a women's health issue. It is an area of concern for many watchdog agencies, including NWLC, Planned Parenthood, NOW, etc. NWLC laments the setbacks incurred because of Gonzales v. Carhart, a Supreme Court decision made in April 2007. By one vote the court upheld a ban on medically approved procedures and excludes exceptions addressing the health of a woman. Justice Ginsberg wrote the dissent, expressing "alarm" at the majority opinion.

Following this "victory" for pro-choice opponents, Congressional leaders supportive of the principles of Roe v. Wade initiated the Freedom of Choice Act in an attempt to codify those principles. Their intention is to support preventive measures and promote better access to contraceptives and comprehensive sex education.

Rates of unintended pregnancy among poor women have caused concern about serious underfunding of publicly funded family planning services, according to the NWLC report. This view is shared by Cecile Richards, president of Planned Parenthood, who says that one billion federal dollars have been wasted on abstinence only programs. At a time when 750,000 U.S. teens will become pregnant and many will contract sexually transmitted diseases, she says it's time for Congress to "get real." Congress should "focus on real solutions for parents and teenagers"(http://www.plannedparent hood.org/about-us/newsroom/press-releases/abstinence-13965.htm). The Planned Parenthood brochure "Six-Step Plan for Increasing the Number of Unintended Pregnancies in America" spotlights a "struggle" going on in America right now between ardent, sometimes zealous, anti-family-planning groups and Planned Parenthood, a pro-choice organization supported in concept by a majority of American people. The brochure claims that these anti-family-planning groups have systematically worked to undermine and block "commonsense measures that could help reduce the number of unintended pregnancies in our country." Planned Parenthood lists a tongue-in-cheek "six-step plan for increasing the number of unintended pregnancies in America":

1. *Keep young people away from real sex education.*

The Bush administration's emphasis on "abstinence only" resulted in millions of dollars being spent on that premise at a time when approximately 750,000 U.S. teens were projected to become pregnant annually, not to mention the huge number of young people expected to contract sexually transmitted diseases! Planned Parenthood lobbied to stop federal funding for the abstinence-only approach, stressing the need for a comprehensive program with "medically accurate sexuality education that discusses both conception and abstinence." The group also promoted passage of the REAL (Responsible Education About Life) Act which emphasizes provision of comprehensive, age-appropriate, and scientifically accurate sexuality education. The REAL Act (Bill #H.R.1653) was introduced in the 110th Congress and was reintroduced in the 111th Congress on March 17, 2009 as H.R. 1551, sponsored by Rep. Barbara Lee (D-CA) along with a hundred co-sponsors; it was then referred to the House Committee on Energy and Commerce. The coordinating Senate Bill S.611, sponsored by Senator Frank Lautenberg (D-NJ) and fifteen co-sponsors, currently remains in the Senate Committee on Health, Education, Labor and Pension.

2. *Put ideology over science and muzzle dissent.*

Planned Parenthood feels that anti-family-planning groups ignore the facts and knowingly plant seeds of misinformation regarding critical topics such as use of condoms. Furthermore, despite government studies indicating that abstinence-only programs have no benefit, the Bush administration continued to seek additional funding and stifled those who disagreed, such as former Attorney General Richard Carmona. Planned Parenthood responded with challenges to the "ideology over science" approach. They put pressure on the FDA, which had "refused to approve over-the-counter access to emergency contraception," caving to "ideological roadblocks" (PP "Six-Step Plan" brochure).

3. *Refuse to dispense birth control at pharmacies.*

Another strategy of the anti-family-planning agitators is to encourage pharmacists to refuse to supply birth control prescriptions to patients. Some pharmacists comply with the religious extremists, empowered by the ultra-conservatives around the country and in Washington, DC. Planned Parenthood representatives pointed out that in nine states legislators introduced eighteen bills allowing pharmacists "to refuse filling birth control prescriptions based on their personal biases." As a result of a nationwide campaign, Planned Parenthood's "Pill Patrol" reached agreements in 2007 with CVS, Rite Aid, Walgreens, and Wal-Mart in which they agreed to a written policy *to fill people's prescriptions for birth control without judgment and without delay.* Target and Winn Dixie are currently in the spotlight because they don't guarantee reproductive rights. Several action-oriented Web sites ask advocates to take action to ensure that women and men have access to quality, affordable reproductive health care. For example, http://www.plannedparenthoodaction.org encourages advocates to remain informed and take appropriate action as necessary. Another site, http://www.unapologeticallyfemale.com/2007/08/activism-idea-planned-parenthood-pill.html, asks us to help "keep pharmacies honest" by visiting them to be certain that there is emergency contraception available and in stock as well as staff members who will honor requests. Activists may sign up and download an activities kit to use for their pharmacy visit and follow-up reports.

4. *Make emergency contraception hard to get.*

Planned Parenthood (PP) states that emergency contraception (EC) is falsely represented as causing abortion when indeed it prevents pregnancy eliminating the need for abortion. After a forty-month effort, PP successfully persuaded the FDA to approve over-the-counter access to EC and continues to battle against the misinformation of anti-family-planning groups.

5. *Keep condom ads off TV.*

FOX and CBS refuse to air condom ads, apparently because they focus on pregnancy prevention rather than on sexually transmitted diseases. PP continues its discussions with the networks and its "Air the Ads" petition campaign. Supporters of Planned Parenthood sent more than 44,000 complaints to the chief executive of CBS and the chairman of entertainment for FOX. Cecile Richards, PP president, feels it is disgraceful that FOX and CBS will sell sex on TV but are unwilling to run ads about prevention of sexually transmitted disease. In addition, Michael Weinstein, president of AIDS Healthcare Foundation, bemoans the fact that we are "hedonistic in our behavior and moralistic in our attitudes" (http://www.nytimes.com/2007/07/16/business/media/16adco.html?_r=1).

6. *Keep family planning services out of the hands of low-income women.*

Planned Parenthood reports that the rate of unintended pregnancy increased by 29 percent among women below the poverty level between 1944 and 2001, contrasted to a 20 percent decline among higher incomes. Title X, America's family planning program for more than thirty years, was kept at level funding by the Bush administration, despite the fact that it serves around five million women unable to afford family planning. Furthermore, Congress added an amendment targeting Planned Parenthood, attempting to disqualify them from Title X funds. Fortunately, that attempt to deny funding was thwarted thanks to a strong, coordinated effort.

We have far to go in the Health and Health Care category, according to the National Women's Law Center. We still have millions without health insurance; there are still no cures for cancers usually associated with women, HMOs and insurance companies control such atrocities as the drive-through mastectomies, and funding for prescription drugs eludes many women. It is shameful that the wealthiest country of the world can't do better for its women and families.

Recent efforts of the Obama administration are providing some optimism for women's health and healthcare. Although the Conservative assault on women's right to choose continues, the current administration has vowed to protect that right. A healthcare bill, Affordable Healthcare for America, has been passed, albeit with many political protestations by those supporting the immense Insurance Lobby and outcries from citizens whose anger was fueled by fear, lies, and half-truths. Signed into law on March 23, 2010 and March 30, 2010 (reconciled) the Health Care Bill is definitely flawed but provides a framework for further tweaking and modification to benefit as many Americans as possible. Women have reasons to feel encouraged.

Workplace Discrepancies and Inequities

It is clear that women have many more job opportunities and career choices than their foremothers did. Women also are better educated today than ever before and are waiting to have families later than in the past.

Newsweek did an issue on women in leadership in its October 15, 2007, edition, citing successful females in various strata of the work world—including CEOs, editors in chief, and college presidents. The Associated Press published an article by Jesse Harlan Alderman on a panel discussion of female Ivy

League college presidents May 3, 2007. Harvard president Drew Gilpin Faust, Brown University president Ruth Simmons, Princeton president Shirley Tilghman, and Judith Rodin, former president of the University of Pennsylvania (now president of the Rockefeller Foundation) met to discuss the status of women in higher education. They applauded the successes of women at the top but expressed concern about the unequal representation of women "in the ranks of tenured faculty at the world's major research universities."

Many women in the focus groups were working women with children and had serious concerns about pay equity and upward mobility. The good news, as we have said, is that there are many more opportunities for females than ever in both traditional and nontraditional areas. There is not-so-good news when it comes to pay parity and upward mobility after the birth of children.

Pay Equity

In the last few years, attention has been paid to discrepancies in salaries garnered by men and women for equal jobs performed. (See appendix, p. 167, for ratios by state.) Fortunately, groups such as AAUW, National Women's Law Center, and MomsRising.org are active watchdogs in this arena.

The AAUW Educational Foundation, recognized for its leadership in research on the educational and economic status of women and girls, released the results of its research in a 2007 report called "Behind the Pay Gap." The research underscored the persistent wage gap between men and women as one that emerges "as early as one year after college graduation" ("Executive Summary," p. 2 <http://www.aauw.org/learn/research/behind PayGap.cfm>) and growing over time. Shortly after graduation, women earn approximately 80 percent of what men earn; after ten years, the percentage falls to approximately 69 percent.

Many people presume that the research does not consider time taken off by women to have babies and raise families, removing them from the employment ranks, and for that reason accept the discrepancy. But the data were determined after controlling for "hours, occupation, parenthood, and other factors known to affect earnings," leaving no apparent explanation for the gap other than gender. The National Women's Law Center corroborates that conclusion, adding that in 2005 "the median annual earnings of women ages 15 and older were $31,858 compared to $41,396 for their male counterparts." Furthermore, statistics for minority women are worse, with African American women earning 64 cents to every dollar earned for equal work performed by a white man and Hispanic women earning a mere 52 cents on the dollar for each dollar given their male counterparts.

According to the AAUW research, this pay gap exists despite the fact that women outperform men in school—earning slightly higher GPAs than men in every college major including science and mathematics (Behind the Pay Gap, p. 10). Catherine Hill, AAUW director of research says, "We need to make the workplaces more family-friendly, reduce sex segregation in education and the workplace, and combat discrimination that continues to hold women back in the workplace" (http://www.msnbc.msn.com/id/18418454/). This sentiment is strongly supported by the organizers of MomsRising.org..

The Motherhood Manifesto, a publication of MomsRising.org, takes the comment even further by saying that there is a deep bias against mothers in America today. Joan Blades and Kristen Rowe-Finkbeiner say that women with children make 73 cents to a man's dollar and single mothers make as little as 60 cents to the man's dollar. They reference a study that indicates that U.S. mothers were 44 percent less likely to be hired than equally qualified non-mothers and "they were offered an average of $11,000 less" (p. 186).

Paycheck Fairness Act

More than forty-five years ago, President Kennedy signed the Equal Pay Act which requires employers to pay the same wages to men and women who perform the same jobs. At that time, women earned only 58 cents to each dollar earned by male counterparts. Although the ratio has improved to approximately 78 cents to the dollar, unequal pay has obviously persisted despite that law. The National Women's Law Center claims that court interpretations of Title VII and the Equal Pay Act were "insufficient to remedy persistent wage disparities." They urged and supported passage of legislation correcting those disparities.

There have been many iterations of The Paycheck Fairness Act, designed to strengthen existing laws and help achieve the goal of parity for equal work performed. Congresswoman Rosa DeLauro in the House, and Hillary Clinton while in the Senate, have worked relentlessly to promote legislation designed to eliminate gender based wage discrimination and ensure that women will finally earn what men earn for doing the same job. According to DeLauro, who introduced the act, the Department of Labor will have the "opportunity to enhance outreach and training programs to work with employers to eliminate pay disparities; employers can share salary information with their co-workers; and women will be allowed to sue for punitive damages in addition to compensatory damages now available under the Equal Pay Act" (http://pr.thinkprogress.org/2008/07/pr20080730/index.html/mobile.html).

The Paycheck Fairness Act has been introduced unsuccessfully numerous times and as of this writing is again being considered by the Senate (S182). One of its objectives, however, was in the spotlight in 2009 with introduction and passage of the Lilly Ledbetter Fair Pay Act, designed to reverse the Supreme Court decision in Ledbetter v. Goodyear Tire and Rubber Co. and to help ensure that "persons subjected to unlawful pay discrimination are able to effectively assert their rights under federal anti-discrimination laws" (NWLC).

Ledbetter had worked nearly twenty years for Goodyear, receiving top performance awards, only to learn that she had been paid significantly less than male counterparts with the same jobs. After her retirement, Lilly sued under Title VII and the Civil Rights Act of 1964 and was awarded back pay and other remedies by a jury. Goodyear appealed, and in Ledbetter v. Goodyear Tire, the Supreme Court held by a 5–4 decision that "employees cannot challenge ongoing compensation discrimination if the employer's original discriminatory decision occurred more than 180 days before, even when the employee continues to receive paychecks that have been discriminatorily reduced."

The NWLC asserts that since pay information is often held confidential, the employee might not realize for a very long time that a pay discrepancy exists. If employers are not held accountable after 180 days, they have little motivation to correct the inequity. The Lilly Ledbetter Fair Pay Act reinstates the former law and promotes employer compliance by holding them accountable to anti-discrimination laws. Employees can challenge paychecks that discriminate based on race, color, national origin, sex, religion, age, or disability.

The Lilly Ledbetter Fair Pay Act was actually passed by the House in the 110th Congress but was defeated by powerful opponents in the Senate, blocking the bill (by three votes) from moving forward. Critics claim that the bill pressures employers to pay employees in predominantly-female jobs with "pleasant working conditions" the same as employees in predominantly-male jobs with "unpleasant conditions." These critics are some of the same fear-mongers distorting the facts of Lilly Ledbetter's case.

Ultimately, the Lilly Ledbetter Fair Pay Act was passed by the 111th Congress in January of 2009 and was the first bill signed into law by President Obama. In his comments, the President said he was happily signing this Act with the future of his daughters in mind. Yes! It is reassuring to know that the president of the United States cares about the rights of women! Passage of the Lilly Ledbetter Act is indeed a victory for women, but as Ledbetter herself commented, passage of the Ledbetter bill without passing the Paycheck Fairness Act is like giving someone a nail without a hammer. The House passed the Paycheck Fairness Act with a bipartisan majority in July 2008, and was passed again in January 2009 with a 256-163 vote. In the Senate, however the Paycheck Fairness Act (S. 182) remains in the Committee on Health, Education, Labor and Pensions. Hearings have been held, but action has not been taken as of August 2010. President Obama and Vice-President Biden have endorsed the Paycheck Fairness Act and have urged the Senate to take action. There is opposition as represented by Michael Steele, Republican National Committee Chairman, and John Boehner of Ohio who claim that the pay equity bill is a "cruehoax." Steele claims it will not empower women but will empower trial lawyers instead (http://content.usa today.com/communities/theoval/post/2010/07/obama-endorses-paycheck-fairness-act/1). Nonetheless, President Obama is ready to sign the bill as soon as the Senate passes it.

As many have indicated, equal pay for women is a family and societal issue. If women's pay were commensurate with men's, the total family income would increase. Many men would be happy to have their family income increase. When women are single-parent supporters of their families, equal pay is not a luxury; it's essential.

Women's Work Issues after Children

People in nearly every focus group mentioned that attitudes definitely change when children enter the picture. According to them, doors close, barriers emerge, and expectations are very different. The authors of *The Motherhood Manifesto* appear to support those claims and fears, as does MomsRising.org generally.

We have made some progress in this area as well, with more women in executive positions and positions of power; but why is it taking so long to pay women the same wage as their male counterparts for the same jobs? When can we pay single mothers a fair wage for their work? Men used to be paid more than women because they were considered "the breadwinners." Female breadwinners are not given the same accommodation.

Politics, Government, and Law

The faces of women are more visible now than ever! The Center for American Women and Politics reports that after the 2008 election there are 91 women out of 535 seats (17 percent) in the House and 17 women out of 100 slots (17 percent) in the Senate. We've had three females as secretary of state, our first female speaker of the house, a viable female candidate for president, and the first Republican female for vice president. President Obama has good female representation in his cabinet, including secretary of state and six (out of twenty) other cabinet or cabinet level positions held by women, as of this writing. While all that is good news, and an improvement from when women were not even allowed to vote, the numbers still do not reflect the ratio of women in political constituencies. In addition, The Center for American Women and Politics reports that, in 2009, 73 women held statewide elective executive posts (23.2 percent of the available 314 positions) across the country and the proportion of women state legislators is 24.3 percent. The progress is commendable, but there is more to be done to further improve the status of women with a more proportional representation in government as well as greater support and sensitivity among males in government positions.

In 2008, for the first time, a woman ran as a viable candidate for U.S. president. She was actually ahead of her male contenders in many of the early polls. Supporters pointed to the fact that Hillary Rodham Clinton was an extremely effective senator, in which capacity she was able to push through more than twenty bills during an extremely divided Congress. Sadly, there are people who admitted that they would never vote for a female candidate for president. At one town meeting, one audience member raised a sign saying, "Iron my shirt!" Such an appalling comment would never have been addressed to a male candidate.

It is reassuring to honor how close a woman came to leading our country, but disconcerting to note that misogynistic tactics were often used in undermining her campaign. We'll consider more on this issue in the next section.

Media Representation of Women

One area of concern common in some degree to all focus groups is how women are represented by the media. It is encouraging to note the trend that we don't often see June Cleaver clones on television any more, and that women are now increasingly portrayed as more independent and intelligent. Representation of females in reality shows, however, is not so real for "normal" people, and is often less than flattering.

Female actors complain that there are very few meaningful roles available for older women; according to them, meaty roles are usually reserved for men, with notable exceptions such as Meryl Streep, Dame Judi Dench, and Helen Mirren! Furthermore, it is the starlets, the beautiful people with beautiful bodies, who are tapped for lucrative productions. There also seems to be a proliferation of Hollywood "bad girls." Media are preoccupied with the antics of Brittany Spears, Lindsay Lohan, poor little rich girl Paris Hilton, and others as paparazzi haunt and hunt these young women to expose their flaws. Sadly these troubled women are held up as "role models" for female tweens and teens.

Some people are taking note of the shortage of meaty leading lady roles for "older" actresses and are taking action, according to "In the Trenches and Over Forty," an article posted at MovieMaker.com on July 20, 2009. Interviewer Rebecca Pahle gets some interesting responses from Debbie Zipp, COO of In the Trenches Productions, a company intent on ensuring fair representation for women in the film industry. In The Trenches Productions produces a wide and diverse range of movie roles for baby boomer women, asserting that women over forty, fifty, sixty, and older are still sexy and powerful. Zipp says that limiting the roles the mature women play is not an honest or true depiction of real life. Those limitations send a subliminal message that women should take a back seat after they reach forty, according to Zipp.

Men don't seem to have the same issues, but Zipp reminds us that the movie industry has been dominated by men since it began. She adds that there are just fewer roles available for women of all ages, compounded by the number of genre movies, such as war movies, comic book and action hero movies, Westerns, etc., with all-male casts. Furthermore, it is common to see an action hero with a much younger woman but rare to see one with a woman of the same age. Zipp claims that "the men running the biz see themselves just as vital and attractive as they were in their youth, and want to keep seeing the women, in their lives or on screen, as being 29!" They view successes in films like *Mama Mia* and *First Wives Club* as anomalies (http://www.moviemaker.com/articles/in_the_trenches_productions_women_over_40_debbie_zipp_20090716/).

But moviemakers cannot ignore the demographic of the spending power of women over forty. Appearance definitely matters in our society. Older women, especially those in the entertainment industry, are reluctant to age gracefully and resort to botox, liposuction, implants, and whatever other product will give them the illusive effects from the elusive fountain of youth. But younger and younger women are resorting to beauty enhancements, such as breast augmentation in teenage years.

Of serious concern is the display of emaciated models that look nothing like "real women," yet are flaunted by the fashion industry and its sponsors. "Skin" is also in. This is an area where I have some ambivalence, as I admit thinking that nakedness in media may be in poor taste; but my attitude was shaped by my generation, influenced by a culture of Victorian thinking, which was in turn influenced by early Christian theologians who portrayed the body as sinful. I need to get over it!

I am amused at the number of women exposing their décolleté even in a work environment. Perhaps it is the influence of fashion. Or perhaps they are simply comfortable in their own skin. The real issue in media exposure seems to be intent, however. If women are portrayed as sex objects to be manipulated and used at the discretion of certain men, then the message is misguided.

The focus groups also point to rap music, along with some cartoons and "shock jock" comments that serve to perpetuate the old patriarchal stereotype of women: ignorant, dependent possessions created for the pleasure of males. Experts support the focus groups' concerns, as we will see below.

Advertisements & Marketing

Susan Douglas, Kellogg Professor of Communication Studies at the University of Michigan, commented on some issues of concern in her 1999 presentation at Tavis, New Mexico. According to the transcript, which sadly remains relevant for today, Dr. Douglas claims that Madison Avenue advertising agencies produce certain images of women which subsequently are refracted through the prism of media. She says that by using "feel good" slogans such as "You've come a long way baby" and "Never underestimate the power of a woman," agencies send mixed messages in camouflage, suggesting that unless you look like the perfection of the supermodel stereotypes you shouldn't expect to succeed. Dr. Douglas also asserts that media overuse stereotypes of women as the unfulfilled professional, nurturing mother, and scheming vixen. She concedes that feminists have made some progress in chipping away at such stereotypes, but we still need to do much more.

Sports Coverage

"(Dis)Empowering Images? Media Representations of Women in Sport," an online article on the Woman Sports Foundation Web site (womenssportsfoundation.org/) provides an interesting perspective on the media representation of women in sports. "Beez" Schell, a PhD in kinesiology with a specialization in women's studies and sociology, acknowledges strides made by females in sports since Title IX—and also expresses her concern at the sexualization of women athletes. Women in sports have been expected to look a certain way. Deviation from that stereotype might lead media to brand a female athlete as lesbian—which at the turn of the millennium was considered a negative.

Dr. Schell cites the influence that media has on girls' and young women's socialization into sports. According to her, media promotes the "ideal look" of white, young, physically attractive, non-disabled women in sports. Such stereotypes may portray sports activities as unattainable to those who do not measure up to the image. She also claims that despite the increased attention given by television, newspapers, and magazines to women's sports, it is offset by increased coverage of men's sports. She is encouraged, however, by the increased popularity of the WNBA, the NCAA Women's Tournament, and USA Women's Soccer, and by the increased promotion of women's sports on cable networks.

Influence of Hip-Hop Culture and Rap Music

The negative representations of women in hip-hop culture and rap music in particular are especially worrisome. In the opinion of many, rap music and the hip-hop culture contribute to the denigration of women and reinforce a false rationale for abuse of women.

In researching information about hip-hop, the culture and the backstory, I came across a very interesting Web site called mysistahs.org and an article originally posted there that was written by a woman identified simply as Ayanna. In her article "The Exploitation of Women in Hip-hop Culture," Ayanna provides a definition and an informative explanation/rationale for the acceptance of hip-hop. She explains that hip-hop culture emanated from black and Latino culture in New York City and includes rapping, singing, deejaying, break-dancing, and graffiti-writing. She adds that the culture has become a lifestyle for young people ages thirteen to thirty and has expanded into music videos, fashion, language, the dance club experience, and "the general way in which young people interact."

Rap music receives wide public attention and has the biggest impact because of its "brutally honest, violent and misogynistic" words, rhythmically chanted over musical renditions. Ayanna makes the point that although hip-hop is often criticized and condemned for its misogynistic message, it has its roots in the broader American culture. Those roots extend back to the days of slavery, during which black women were either raped or expected to provide their sexual skills with any man desiring them. They were baby factories providing new workers for the slave masters, and sexuality was their only recognized value. That stereotype of an oversexed, promiscuous black woman has persisted for many centuries. As a result Ayanna maintains that, sadly, many women define their value by what they can do for men. Because of that poor self-concept, many black women "consent and collaborate" with sexual exploitation.

Ayanna does not support censorship as a means to keep rap and hip-hop in check, but maintains that instead we must change the culture. Once again, education is the only way to effect such a change. She says, "People need to be aware that women's rights are being violated verbally in the sexist lyrics, in physical interactions at the hip-hop events, and in the general way that hip-hop youth interact with one another every day." It is only in awareness of such abuse and its history that we can begin to implement change (http:// thestudyofracialism.org/post-27351.html).

Further information on rap and hip-hop comes from staff writer Dana Williams, writing a first article in the series "Misogyny in Music: What Teens Think" in a year-long project for Tolerance.org (http://www.tolerance.org/ news/article_tol.jsp?id=941, accessed February 11, 2007). To demonstrate vividly the kind of language that expresses alleged misogyny, Williams cites lyrics from the song "Drips" from the album "The Eminem Show." The lyrics refer with crude inflection to kicking a pregnant woman in the stomach and throwing her off a porch because her behavior is begging for the use of that kind of force (http://www.metrlyrics.com/drips-lyrics-eminem.html).

"Drips" won a Grammy as part of the best rap album in 2003, despite its promotion of hatred and violence against women. Williams claims that although Eminem has received some negative feedback for such presenta- tions, he is just one of many performers who use such language. Although some in the music industry argue that this is artists' creative use of free speech, critics feel that society pays a huge price.

It is a very high price indeed, according to Dr. Gwendolyn Pough, assis- tant professor of women's studies at the University of Minnesota. Pough, an expert in "women, rap, and the hip-hop feminism," says that such lyrics have had a serious impact especially on young black women. Those misogynistic messages inform the mind and frame the behavior for women who have little self-worth. Furthermore, dating violence and forced sexual behavior appear to be condoned as the norm, according to Dr. Michael Rich, a pediatrician at Children's Hospital in Boston quoted in Dana Williams' article. As spokesperson for the American Academy of Pediatrics' "Media Matters" campaign, Rich says: "Media are a source of information and a source where young people learn about relationships." According to Rich, there is a strong association between behavior and the misogynistic lyrics of rap, even if it may not be the total explanation for the behavior.

In 2007 Marvin Mills posted some relevant comments in "Hip-hop: America's Mirror" (laloyolan.com) and proclaims that he is "hip-hop and always will be." He describes hip-hop music as "an extension of the world it talks about which the listeners and artists collaborate to form."

Mills endorses and supports the genre in general and derides discussions conducted by Congress' House subcommittees on Commerce, Trade, and Consumer Protection. The congressional hearing, entitled "From Imus to Industry: The business of stereotypes and degrading images," focused on "media, stereotypes, and degradation of women." Mills complains that Congress seems to put as much emphasis on hip-hop as it does on weapons of mass destruction. He admits that current hip-hop music and videos have negative issues such as exploitation of women and focus on materialism and sex, but according to him such portrayals ironically reflect the "struggle and negativity that looms in the actual neighborhoods of its artists." When America changes, so will hip-hop, according to Marvin Mills (October 18, 2007: http://www.laloyolan.com/opinion/hip-hop-america-s-mirror-1.394959).

Some Spelman College students let their voices be heard in 2004 when they rejected rap artist Nelly's bone-marrow drive after he refused to attend a forum in which students could question him about his then-current video for the song "Tip Drill." Spelman, located in Atlanta, Georgia, prides itself on its all black female student body. Their decision to reject Nelly's event was difficult, as the bone-marrow cause is very critical; but the students felt that the depiction of women in his video was so offensive that their action was warranted. Reports indicate that the video could only be shown on BET's "Uncut" in the wee hours because of the nearly nude dancing women and the act of swiping a credit card on a woman.

In the following year, Spelman sponsored a hip-hop week to investigate the impact of hip-hop in urban, suburban, and rural communities and the exploitation of women in the music industry. Janelle Richards and Nisa Islam

Muhammad report that the college sponsored the events to listen to aspiring artists and to view a screening of "Masculinity in Hip Hop." There were many opportunities to reflect on the significance of the genre, and some concluded that rap could also represent positive things and should be considered a medium for the younger generation.

Persistent Stereotypes

A section on gender at mediaknowall.com contends that media representation of women is a constant concern. The writers question whether the status of women has really changed or whether the male-dominated media do not want it to change. The article "Gender and Media Representation" (http://www.mediaknowall.com/as_alevel/alevel.php?pageID=gender), says that media tend to focus on the following as representations of women:

- beauty, narrowly defined
- size/physique, within parameters
- sexuality, based on beauty and body
- emotional rather than intellectual activities
- relationships, rather than independence and freedom

The section concludes by saying that media represent women by their physical attributes to the near exclusion of other values. It points to the lack of powerful female role models and "the extremely artificial nature of such portrayals, which bear little or no relation to women across the planet." This information lends credence to concerns mentioned above.

Adelina Herrarte also discusses this topic in an article entitled "Panel discusses mass media representations of women," published by *Washington Square News* (posted March 11, 1999, http://www.nyunews.com). Students attending the event were divided into groups, provided with magazines, and asked to find women represented in positive ways. Although one Latina magazine portrayed a woman dressed in a professional suit as if ready for business, most other representations were not viewed positively by participants. Many were unhappy with the "media's unrealistic portrayal of the ideal woman as thin, sexy, and beautiful." They said they couldn't necessarily blame the publishers exclusively since obviously, "Sex sells."

And finally, a Media Awareness Network article, "Beauty and Body Image in the Media," says that unrealistic standards of beauty are being imposed on women—most of whom are larger and more mature than any of the models they see in TV ads and magazines. The article claims that promotion of such standards is largely economic, no big surprise. Women insecure about their bodies view those ads and are enticed to purchase new clothes, beauty products, diet aids, etc. It is in the best interest of the businesses to promote thinness, and to present an ideal difficult to achieve and maintain. They are thus assured of constant purchases of their products and services! (http://www.media-awareness.ca/english/issues/stereotyping/women_and_ girls/women_beauty.cfm).

Use of Sexist Language

We need to acknowledge the use of sexist language in media. Perhaps we can be a little "touchy" about words that we feel are "politically incorrect" and overreact. Why does it matter?

During the Women's Liberation Movement of the sixties and seventies, sensitivities were raised about words that are demeaning to women. After all, even words like mankind, history, etc., implied that women don't matter. We did become obsessed with finding more gender-neutral words. Waitresses and waiters were replaced by servers; workman was replaced by worker; stewardess was replaced by flight attendant, and so on. Manhole cover was a bit more challenging.

Sherryl Kleinman writes in "Why Sexist Language Matters" (March 12, 2007, Alternet.org) that gendered words and phrases like "you guys" may seem petty when compared to big issues like domestic violence against women, but that simple language changes might help in our efforts to overcome gender inequality. Ms. Kleinman, a professor of sociology at the University of North Carolina, Chapel Hill, teaches a course on gender inequality. Her course includes wage gap issues, equalization of women's worth with physical attractiveness, sexual harassment, physical violence against women, and such.

In discussing such behavior, she says that men and women in her classes have the most difficult time understanding—or perhaps, as she believes "share a strong unwillingness to understand"—sexist language. Professor Kleinman defends her sensitivity by saying that "male-based generics are another indicator—and more importantly a reinforcer—of a system in which 'man' in the abstract and men in the flesh are privileged over women." She responds to her detractors by saying that if language is a reflection of reality then perhaps it's time to pay attention to the words we use and help change the reality.

There are many words she draws to the reader's attention, but she is especially perplexed by the prolific use of "you guys." According to her, it might make women feel good to be considered "one of the guys"; but it is only a "pretense of inclusion." She campaigns to change the phrase to "you all," which is not gender specific, claiming that even small changes such as that can begin to change the way we think. "You all" sounds "region specific" to me, but I get her point.

Impact of "Shock Jocks"

Along with some rap lyrics, words used by so-called shock jocks are the most outrageous examples of media abuse of women and sexist language. Don Imus was fired under pressure from radio advertisers after he called the Rutgers women's basketball team "rough girls" and "nappy-headed hos." He ultimately apologized to the team personally for his poor judgment and explained that he was only using language that hip-hop music uses. Many people were outraged by his behavior, but he was subsequently hired by another radio channel after a suitable hiatus.

In her podcasts, Dr. Joanna Lipari describes "current events from a psychological point of view." In "Don Imus: Shock Jock Shock" (April 11, 2007), she claims that Imus, Ann Coulter, Rush Limbaugh, and Howard Stern wouldn't make such outrageous comments unless they had an audience that wants to hear them.

That view is also supported by Rebecca Vesely, West Coast bureau chief of *Women's eNews*. According to Vesely, Tom Leykis is a shock jock of a syndicated talk show whose audience includes listeners in San Francisco, Detroit,

Vancouver, and Dallas. His large male audience, young and white, ranks third (regionally) in the target market of men aged 18–44 according to Arbitron ratings. Vesely says that Leykis follows in the tradition of Howard Stern, making a fortune by "reducing women and men to cartoonish, sex-obsessed versions of themselves."

According to Vesely, men in Leykis' world pursue women for sex while women seek to control men and spend their money. She cites critics who claim that Leykis is worse than Stern with his more mean-spirited and misogynistic view of women for entertainment's sake. Critics blame the popularity of the show for why Leykis does it that way—as part of an emerging trend to prioritize ratings over standards for language. Once again it is the bottom-line "buck" that informs profit-driven media conglomerates who "are more interested in delivering viewers to advertisers than in serving the needs of the public" (January 6, 2003, Women's eNews, "Radio Shock Jock Pushes Limits of Sexist Gab").

In contrast to that kind of popularity, I'd like to mention again the valiant presidential campaign of Hillary Rodham Clinton. Clinton reported "eighteen million cracks in the glass ceiling" as a result of her bid for office. She had, after all, received more than eighteen million votes in primaries across the country.

Many of Senator Clinton's supporters were critical of the sexist language used in media coverage throughout her campaign. According to Mary Douglas Vavrus in her book *Postfeminist News*, "Hillary Rodham Clinton seems to inspire a mixture of respect and disdain from media personnel, and this mixture is more often than not structured by patterned references that reveal their creators' perspectives on women, power, and public life."

Despite Senator Clinton's incredible experience and leadership, she has been described as "overly ambitious," "a woman people love to hate," and "calculating" to name a few. According to Ashleigh Crowther in "Sexist Language in Media Coverage of Hillary Clinton" (December, 12, 2007, mediacrit.wetpaint.com), the media perpetuates an image of Clinton as "scary" or "intimidating." Media underscored that characterization by making a caricature of her laugh, which was captured in a sound bite played over and over again, not just by late-night comics and conservative talk show hosts but also by mainstream television and radio. This "cackle," as they described it, was consistent with "evil sounding laughter," "the laugh of witches," according to Crowther.

The press was also more concerned with cleavage, pantsuits, and hairstyles than in listening to the substance of Clinton's issues. The negative female stereotypes applied to Senator Clinton reflected the sexist and sometimes misogynistic biases of the media.

Then along came Sarah! At the 2008 Republican National Convention, the GOP candidate for president, John McCain, surprised the nation by announcing that his running mate for vice-president would be Sarah Palin, governor of Alaska. Many praised the selection of a female candidate for VP, and Governor Palin's charisma excited and charged both the convention and the Republican party. Many women struggled, however, with the pistol packing, pro-war, anti-choice rhetoric of this mother of five and were ambivalent about her candidacy. But feminists along with supporters of Governor Palin noted that she, too, was treated with the same sexism and misogynistic nuance that Senator Clinton had endured. The press attacked Mrs. Palin's perceived lack of experience but were just as concerned about her wardrobe and the amount of money spent to support her new image.

The focus groups were right on the money here: Since media have such a huge influence on all age, ethnic, and economic groups, reporters, commentators, pundits, and the interests they represent need to do some soul-searching about how they perpetuate negative biases against women. The 2008 presidential campaign was certainly revealing. Just as many failed to pursue and report the truths of the war in Iraq, much of the media failed to remain unbiased in the election campaign and de facto influenced how some people voted. But there was a victory of sorts, perhaps not specifically for women but for humankind with the election of an African American man. History was made and a barrier was broken.

Should we consider the election of Barack Obama as an encouraging sign for women? We can only be hopeful that as a victorious minority male, the husband of an intelligent female lawyer, and a father of two young daughters, President Obama will continue to be sensitive to the plights of women in America and prioritize our issues. Signing into law the Lilly Ledbetter Fair Pay Act was a clear indication of his good will. Furthermore, in March 2009 the President signed an executive order establishing a White House

Council on Women and Girls whose mission will be "to provide a coordinated federal response to the challenges confronted by women and girls to ensure that all Cabinet and Cabinet-level agencies consider how their policies and programs impact women and families." That action in itself appears to be very encouraging, but some of the outrage expressed in blogs against the decision is frightening!

Musings on the Report Card

So how did women do on our report card? Not very well, I'm afraid; but the glass is half full. Significant steps and building blocks were made as a result of the Women's Rights Movement in the sixties and seventies. Some of those gains suffered setbacks in recent years, with assaults on Roe v. Wade and a woman's right to choose.

Although women now hold positions they've never held before, the glass ceiling still exists. The wage gap persists, despite efforts by some to equalize pay for males and females doing the same work.

Women are treated as partners in some homes, but remain subservient in far too many. Divorce, on the other hand, carries fewer stigmas than it used to. Domestic abuse still exists in unacceptable numbers.

Health care is still not available for millions of women and men; there are no cures for breast and ovarian cancer, although a preventative inoculation has been developed for cervical cancer. (The inoculation is controversial, however, as conservatives feel it condones sexuality. The Human Papillomavirus is the highly contagious, sexually transmitted virus believed to be the most common cause of cervical cancer, and inoculation must be given to boys and girls before they become sexually active.)

Blatant and latent sexist and misogynistic attitudes still exist in words and deeds both in the media and in everyday life.

On a positive note, there is a greater representation of women in elected office and hopefully that percentage will continue to increase.

Our focus groups had some mixed forecasts for the future, but many of them offered some optimism.

Status of Women in the Future

What does the future hold for women in the U.S.? By 2017 will females achieve balance with their male counterparts and partners, or at least improve their current status? Focus groups weighed in on possible futures with mixed reviews, depending on the emerging leadership and economy of this country.

New England participants were fairly optimistic, qualifying their optimism for some responses by confidence that there would be a new administration in Washington, D.C., and a reduction of war commitments. Some responses were contradictory across the groups and were not necessarily unanimous but garnered enough support to be included. It was not pragmatic to list their "forecasts" in the six generic categories we established earlier, as items often overlapped. Participants felt that by 2017 . . .

- More women will be more comfortable with their own bodies and have greater acceptance.

- There will be more appropriate role models because of awareness campaigns.

- There will be an increased possibility for a female president.

- More women will hold prominent business positions.

- We will witness a thinning, but not an elimination of the glass ceiling.

- Emotional intelligence will be valued.

- There will be a reduction of stereotypes in career issues.

- Alternate health care solutions will be available.

- Cures for breast and ovarian cancer will be found.

- Generation Y females are better educated, but engagement of young women is uncertain.

- Less rigorous curricula (dumbing down) will be employed.

- There will be a possibility of violence and backlash against women's accomplishments (power and control issues).

Oregon participants tended to be more pessimistic, forecasting a possible collapse of the physical environment and an economic collapse that will greatly impact women. They also predicted that part-time jobs will provide flexibility for a balanced life for women, but will offer no job security—clearly a two-edged sword.

Florida participants were unclear about the future. They expressed hope that women will be stronger and in influential positions of power. They also said that while some women will postpone marriage and family until a career is established, some would still rely on a man to support them, and in some cases remain in abusive relationships.

Although not confident enough to forecast that all objectives could be accomplished by 2017, some participants also included items for a "wish list." They named the following:

- Equal pay for equal work

- Universal health care for all

- Females in areas seemingly forbidden to women, such as U.S. president, Catholic priests, etc.

- Better childcare opportunities for all; public pre-school

- Eradication of poverty in this country

- Change in narratives of language, e.g., mistress/master

Gender balance was the ultimate wish for all groups, but the presence of more ladies' rooms in public places was also included. (Ladies' rooms have longer lines than men's rooms.) This is one area where women wanted more! They might just get their wish if the House Oversight and Government Reform Committee supports the "Potty Parity Act." The bill, H.R. 4869. IH, seeks to address the number of restroom facilities for women in federal buildings by requiring a one-to-one ratio for toilets, including urinals, in women's and men's restrooms. Now that is a bill we can smile about! (http://www.washingtonpost.com/wp-dyn/content/article/2010/05/12/AR2010051205038_pf.html).

How many of these wishes can become realities? Clearly there is much to be done!

The focus groups also suggested strategies for achieving a better balance of opportunity between men and women. It appears that most of their recommendations involve education, increasing awareness, and engagement of both young women and men:

- Curricula must be modified from kindergarten through high school to include information about women's issues, women's history, etc.

- Greater emphasis needs to be given to women's worth, along with their contributions and value to society. Show the benefits of "equality."

- Teach women salary negotiation skills and positioning strategies for upward mobility,

- Women need to learn about empowerment without entitlement, according to some. (Generation Y women are perceived as feeling entitled without being willing to fight for rights as predecessors have done.)

- Develop better curriculum standards for health, technology, etc.

- Include values in curriculum planning.

- Emphasize and value service to others through service learning, etc.

- Teach women to organize themselves to best represent their needs and issues.

- Reduce complacency about voting.

- Increase awareness about loss of rights.

- Provide better recognition for female artists through awareness and information campaigns.

- Engage men in the process whenever possible/appropriate.

The focus groups also recommended, with respect to social services:

- Redefine roles in marriage/partnerships for better balance.

- Encourage activism among younger men and women to achieve better gender balance.

Although the future projections of the focus groups are generally encouraging, so much depends upon the political course of the country and the officials we elect. We are on the threshold of change, poised to tip in one direction or another. We are currently in the throes of a "conservative" influence that asserts its often-dogmatic agenda rooted in its philosophy that "people get what they deserve." But who determines what "they" deserve?

New Justices will impact Supreme Court decisions. In 2009 President Obama nominated Sonia Sotomayor to replace retiring Justice David Souter. After Senate confirmation in August 2009, she became the first Latina Justice of the U.S. Supreme Court. The President's next opportunity to nominate a replacement came when Justice John Paul Stevens announced his plans to retire in June, 2010. The Obama nominee, fifty-year-old U.S. Solicitor General Elena Kagan, was confirmed by the Senate on August 6, 2010, by a 63–37 vote. The vote was mostly along party lines, with some crossover votes, denying a filibuster. Kagan will be the fourth woman to serve as a Supreme Court Justice and for the first time women will comprise one-third of the Supreme Court. Conservative Republicans had vowed, however, to oppose any nominees they perceived to be Progressive. What impact, if any, will the new composition of the nation's highest court have on future decisions? How will it impact future challenges to Roe v. Wade? Will three women on the highest court make a difference?

Will we provide adequate health care, or will women and children continue to suffer the consequences of electing shortsighted legislators? A Health Care Bill was signed into law in March 2010 but is considered too weak by some progressives and too expensive by conservatives. Many feel that the bill is at least a beginning. Time will tell.

Tax rebates awarded by the Bush administration were hailed as a stimulus to the economy. Rapidly escalating fuel and gas prices quickly consumed a chunk of those checks. We didn't know then what lay ahead.

How long will the wars in Iraq and Afghanistan continue? Between the billions spent on wars and the money we've borrowed from China and elsewhere to finance them, our economy has been seriously challenged. In addition, manipulation by powerful banks, the greed of CEOs, and so-called Ponzi schemes cheating investors out of billions of dollars have all contributed to the further decline and current crisis in our economy. When the bottom dropped out of the economy, millions of people were faced with foreclosure, bankruptcies, and other hardships, again because of greed on the part of banks and financial institutions. Also at fault were those agencies charged with monitoring the actions of those institutions.

The Obama administration must pick up the pieces and make some difficult choices to bring this country back to solvency and greatness. Sadly, there was so much hope and promise for improving social programs, helping those who need it most, and bolstering the middle class, but many of those policy changes will have to wait until the president and Congress can harness the recession beast and pull us out of the ashes.

All these issues threaten programs needed to improve the lot for women and children, especially those who are poor and working poor. It was recently reported that with an unemployment rate either in or approaching double digits in many parts of the country, more men than women are being laid off. The explanation offered was that women are often in the lower paying jobs. What does this tell us?

We are fortunate that many watchdog agencies and committed public servants are doing their best to increase awareness about women's issues, to implement change and where appropriate take action to ameliorate setbacks that are detrimental to the well-being of women and families.

We can be cautiously optimistic, but achieving what women want their futures to look like depends to some extent upon our investment of time, effort, and passion. Even when the economy improves, changes won't come easily. Women have many choices to make, with no guarantees, but at least making conscious efforts improve the chances to accomplish desired change. Apathy guarantees the status quo or worse.

Choice seems to be the operative word in women's rights issues. In a sweet movie about women's suffrage, an older woman argued that since her husband voted, she didn't need to vote; she could influence him in her own ways. A younger suffragette responded that voting shouldn't be a requirement but a choice!

There is a desperate need to re-ignite passion for equality. Wealthy and highly educated women will handle challenges, but what about women who are poor and oppressed?

Concluding Remarks

The vestiges of Eve remain. Eve is surely a part of our cellular memories. Whether you are religious, spiritual, or non-religious, fundamentalist or progressive in your beliefs, women have borne the stigma and guilt for far too long. Female self-concepts have been assaulted for more than three millennia and the effects will be difficult to dismantle. Women have been considered property, slaves, and playthings. We have allowed ourselves to be second-class citizens because we bought in to the concept that we don't deserve better.

Fortunately, there have been women who broke chains and led the way to truth. We have much to learn from them, including better self-concepts without guilt, fear, and self-deprecation. We need to help other women get ahead and move beyond the glass ceiling, putting aside petty jealousies. There will no doubt continue to be the Phyllis Schlaflys of the world and fundamentalists who maintain that women are intended by God to be in support positions, subservient to men. For those who choose that path, that is their option; but for those who seek equality with male counterparts in relationships, business, and church status, that should truly be their choice. Piece by piece, person by person, we can chip away at the myth and change the collective consciousness.

Where do you stand? Do you care? What action can you as an individual take to help males and females achieve parity and balance? Let me make some suggestions based on some focus group recommendations.

Educate Yourself and Others

Be Aware (Beware): Pay attention to issues affecting women and women's rights. Attend seminars and programs designed to increase awareness about the status of women. Better yet, bring a friend and share what you learn with your peers. Read articles in the media and online dealing with gender equity. Watch the actions and voting patterns of your elected officials and observe whether or not they support women's rights. Political activism may be viewed on a spectrum of involvement. You don't have to run for office or work on a political campaign, but at the very least don't support candidates and officials who want to take away your rights and diminish your status.

Be Engaged in Your Own Destiny

Take action in some of the following areas:

- Set up and/or participate in blogs and other effective means of communication designed to encourage dialogue and discourse on women's issues: the good, the bad, and the ugly.

- Celebrate victories and denounce losses undermining women's rights.

- Take a stand and protest outrageous behaviors and legislation against women.

- Vote for those supporting gender equity.

- Mentor younger females.

- Include history/herstory of women and our achievements in curricula of appropriate disciplines.

Enlist the Support of Males

By all means engage men in the process, increasing their awareness of women's rights, and encouraging their participation in achieving gender balance and fairness. Pay equity, for example, is in the best interest of family economics and solvency since many working wives/partners contribute heavily to the family budget. Paying a woman less than her male counterpart not only cheats the woman, it cheats the family. The recent signing into law of the Lilly Ledbetter Fair Pay Act (2009) is a step in the right direction and worthy of celebration. Unfortunately there will be some who will attempt to avoid compliance.

Do something!! As cited at the beginning of this chapter, Louise Otto Peters has told us that "women will be forgotten if they forget to think about themselves." If you choose, you can start your action plan by sharing additional suggestions and experiences on my Web site: www.melindarising.com. I welcome your creative approaches and new ideas. As sisters of Eve, let's move forward out of the darkness and let her rest in peace!

Appendix
AAUW: Breaking though Barriers

Median earnings for and earnings ratio between male and female full-time, year-round workers, ages 16 and older, all educational levels, by state

	Men	Women	Earnings Ratio	Rank
Alabama	$41,411	$30,681	74%	37
Alaska	$51,500	$37,861	74%	42
Arizona	$41,524	$34,556	83%	3
Arkansas	$36,839	$27,487	75%	33
California	$47,758	$40,521	85%	2
Colorado	$47,270	$36,618	77%	17
Connecticut	$58,838	$44,625	76%	26
Delaware	$46,898	$37,049	79%	13
Dist. of Columbia	$57,393	$50,519	88%	1
Florida	$40,672	$32,506	80%	9
Georgia	$42,391	$34,513	81%	7
Hawaii	$45,577	$36,709	81%	8
Idaho	$41,461	$29,730	72%	45
Illinois	$50,022	$36,968	74%	41
Indiana	$44,906	$31,935	71%	47
Iowa	$41,677	$31,903	77%	22
Kansas	$43,346	$32,066	74%	40
Kentucky	$40,977	$31,089	76%	25
Louisiana	$43,326	$29,147	67%	49
Maine	$40,908	$32,613	80%	10
Maryland	$53,189	$44,188	83%	4

	Men	Women	Earnings Ratio	Rank
Massachusetts	$55,555	$43,452	78%	16
Michigan	$48,720	$35,260	72%	43
Minnesota	$48,637	$37,281	77%	21
Mississippi	$37,436	$27,697	74%	38
Missouri	$42,106	$31,820	76%	31
Montana	$38,440	$29,634	77%	18
Nebraska	$40,860	$30,885	76%	29
Nevada	$45,178	$34,724	77%	19
New Hampshire	$51,655	$36,946	72%	46
New Jersey	$55,980	$44,343	79%	12
New Mexico	$40,359	$30,623	76%	24
New York	$48,882	$40,490	83%	5
North Carolina	$40,875	$32,397	79%	11
North Dakota	$41,249	$29,589	72%	44
Ohio	$45,214	$33,628	74%	34
Oklahoma	$39,860	$30,123	76%	30
Oregon	$43,226	$33,959	79%	14
Pennsylvania	$46,455	$35,265	76%	23
Rhode Island	$49,265	$36,536	74%	36
South Carolina	$40,998	$31,063	76%	28
South Dakota	$37,493	$28,431	76%	27
Tennessee	$40,458	$31,091	77%	20
Texas	$41,539	$32,530	78%	15
Utah	$45,028	$31,183	69%	48
Vermont	$41,778	$34,424	82%	6
Virginia	$50,203	$37,859	75%	32
Washington	$51,272	$37,932	74%	39
West Virginia	$40,941	$27,472	67%	50
Wisconsin	$45,266	$33,640	74%	35
Wyoming	$48,555	$31,204	64%	51
Puerto Rico	$19,942	$20,165	101%	n/a

	Men	Women	Earnings Ratio
United States*	$46,367	$35,745	77%

Median earnings for and earnings ratio between male and female full-time, year-round workers, ages 16 and older, all educational levels, by state Sources: U.S. Census Bureau, American Community Survey, 2008; and Puerto Rico Community Survey, 2008.

*National data based on Current Population Survey data, U.S. Census Bureau. Source: Income, Poverty, and Health Insurance Coverage in the United States: 2008 (September, 2009).

Median earnings for and earnings ratio between male and female full-time, year-round college-educated workers, ages 25 and older, by state

	Men	Women	Earnings Ratio	Rank
Alabama	$65,000	$45,000	69%	41
Alaska	$70,000	$45,000	64%	51
Arizona	$66,000	$48,000	73%	21
Arkansas	$58,000	$41,000	71%	35
California	$80,000	$60,000	75%	10
Colorado	$71,000	$50,000	70%	37
Connecticut	$82,000	$61,000	74%	14
Delaware	$70,000	$52,000	74%	15
Dist. of Columbia	$85,000	$68,000	80%	3
Florida	$60,000	$45,000	75%	10
Georgia	$69,500	$50,000	72%	28
Hawaii	$60,000	$50,000	83%	2
Idaho	$59,000	$43,000	73%	20
Illinois	$72,000	$51,000	71%	33
Indiana	$65,000	$46,000	71%	34
Iowa	$59,000	$42,400	72%	29
Kansas	$60,000	$44,000	73%	18
Kentucky	$60,000	$45,000	75%	10
Louisiana	$64,000	$42,600	67%	50
Maine	$58,900	$40,400	69%	45
Maryland	$83,000	$61,000	73%	17
Massachusetts	$80,000	$58,000	73%	25
Michigan	$70,000	$52,000	74%	15
Minnesota	$70,000	$50,000	71%	30
Mississippi	$56,300	$40,000	71%	32
Missouri	$62,000	$43,000	69%	40
Montana	$50,000	$40,000	80%	3
Nebraska	$58,000	$42,000	72%	27
Nevada	$62,000	$48,000	77%	7
New Hampshire	$73,000	$50,000	68%	46
New Jersey	$85,000	$60,000	71%	36

	Men	Women	Earnings Ratio	Rank
New Mexico	$64,000	$45,000	70%	38
New York	$73,000	$57,000	78%	6
North Carolina	$65,000	$45,000	69%	41
North Dakota	$55,000	$40,000	73%	21
Ohio	$67,000	$49,000	73%	19
Oklahoma	$60,000	$40,000	67%	49
Oregon	$65,000	$49,000	75%	9
Pennsylvania	$70,000	$50,000	71%	30
Rhode Island	$70,000	$55,000	79%	5
South Carolina	$60,000	$42,000	70%	39
South Dakota	$50,000	$37,200	74%	13
Tennessee	$64,000	$44,000	69%	44
Texas	$70,000	$47,800	68%	47
Utah	$65,000	$45,000	69%	41
Vermont	$62,100	$45,000	72%	26
Virginia	$82,000	$55,000	67%	48
Washington	$73,000	$53,000	73%	24
West Virginia	$55,000	$40,000	73%	21
Wisconsin	$63,000	$48,000	76%	8
Wyoming	$54,000	$48,000	89%	1

	Men	Women	Earnings Ratio
United States*	$70,000	$50,000	70%

Source: American Community Survey, the U.S. Census Bureau. Data compiled and analyzed for AAUW by JSI Associates. For more information about JSI Associates, visit www.jobsearchintelligence.com.

Note: The analysis includes all workers who worked at least 35 hours/week, year-round, including teachers who were defined as "year-round" workers if they worked 40 weeks or more per year. (For other workers, "year-round" is defined as working 48 weeks or more annually.) Median earnings for male and female full-time workers were calculated using data from the 2008 public use micro-sample (PUMS) of the American Community Survey (ACS).

Bibliography

Acocella, Joan. "The Saintly Sinner: The two-thousand-year obsession with Mary Magdalene," in *Secrets of Mary Magdalene*, ed. Dan Burstein & Arne J. De Keijzer (New York: CDS Books, 2006) 37–54.

Beavis, Bill & McCloskey, Richard. *Salty Dog Talk: The Nautical Origins of Everyday Expressions*. London: Adlard Coles Nautical, 2007.

Blades, Joan & Rowe-Finkbeiner, Kristin. *The Motherhood Manifesto: What America's Moms Want—and What to Do about It*. New York: Nation Books, 2006.

Brock, Ann Graham. *Mary Magdalene, the First Apostle: The Struggle for Authority*. Cambridge, MA: Harvard University Press, 2003.

Brown, Dan. *The DaVinci Code*. New York: Doubleday, 2003.

Burstein, Dan & De Keijzer, Arne J., eds. *Secrets of Mary Magdalene*. New York: CDS Books, 2006.

Campbell, Joseph. *The Power of Myth*. New York: Anchor Books, 1991.

Carroll, James. "Who Was Mary Magdalene?" in *Secrets of Mary Magdalene*, ed. Dan Burstein & Arne J. De Keijzer (New York: CDS Books, 2006) 21–36.

Flinders, Carol Lee. *At the Root of this Longing: Reconciling a Spiritual Hunger and a Feminine Thirst*. San Francisco: HarperSanFrancisco, 1998.

Friedan, Betty. *The Feminine Mystique*. New York: W.W. Norton & Company, 2001.

Gage, Matilda Joslyn. *Woman, Church and State*. Salem, NH: Ayer Company Publishers, Inc, 1992 (reprint).

Haskins, Susan. *Mary Magdalen: Myth and Metaphor*. New York: Harper Collins, 1993.

Johnson, Paul. *A History of Christianity*. New York: Touchstone, 1995.

King, Karen L. "The Gospel of Mary," in *Secrets of Mary Magdalene*, ed. Dan Burstein

& Arne J. De Keijzer (New York: CDS Books, 2006) 102–106.

Lerner, Robert. *The Heresy of the Free Spirit in the Later Middle Ages.* Berkeley, CA: University of California Press, 1972.

McGowan, Kathleen. "Mary Magdalene, Superstar," in *Secrets of Mary Magdalene,* ed. Dan Burstein & Arne J. De Keijzer (New York: CDS Books, 2006) 283–289.

Pagels, Elaine. *Adam, Eve, and the Serpent.* New York: Vintage, 1989.

————. *Beyond Belief: The Secret Gospel of Thomas.* New York: Random House, 2003.

————. *The Gnostic Gospels.* New York: Vintage, 1989.

Pelikan, Jaroslav. *Mary through the Centuries: Her Place in the History of Culture.* New Haven, CT and London, England: Yale University Press, 1996.

Picknett, Lynn & Prince, Clive. *The Templar Revelation: Secret Guardians of the True Identity of Christ.* New York: Touchstone, 1997.

Ralls, Karen. *Knights Templar Encyclopedia: The Essential Guide to the People, Places, Events and Symbols of the Order of the Temple.* Franklin Lakes, NJ: New Page Books, 2007.

Starbird, Margaret. *The Woman with the Alabaster Jar: Mary Magdalen and the Holy Grail.* Rochester, VT: Bear & Company, 1993.

Stone, Merlin. *When God Was a Woman.* New York: Harcourt Brace & Company, 1976.

Torjesen, Karen Jo. *When Women Were Priests.* New York: Harper Collins, 1995.

Walker, Barbara G. *The Woman's Dictionary of Symbols and Sacred Objects.* New York: Harper Collins Publishers, 1988.

Walker, Barbara G. *The Woman's Encyclopedia of Myths and Secrets.* San Francisco: HarperSanFrancisco, 1983.

Warner, Marina. *Alone of All Her Sex: The Myth and the Cult of the Virgin Mary.* New York: Vintage, 1983.

Index